You're Too Young*

Vincent M. Vassolo

Creative Director

Copywriter

M.S., Clinical Gerontology
Post-Graduate Professional Certificate, Gerontology Counseling

* But You Can Learn To "Think Old" And Profit

From The Lucrative Baby Boomer Market

Acknowledgment

Thanks to my son Michael V. Vassolo (he's the Vigor in Vim, Vigor & Vassolo LLC, an agency that specializes in advertising and marcom for the Baby Boomer market). In addition to serving as editor of this book, he also helped formulate and refine the concepts throughout, bringing clarity to issues that I often found confusing. Without his skillful help, this book wouldn't have been possible. Of course, I take full responsibility for any errors, omissions or just plain boneheaded mistakes that I may have let slip through.

Dedication

To Vincent R. Vassolo, my father and the creator of the Maytag Loneliest Man In Town for Leo Burnett. Without his mentoring, I wouldn't know a damn thing about advertising.

And to James W. Ellor, a pioneer in the study of aging, who patiently guided me throughout my education in clinical gerontology.

Table of Contents

Please Allow Me
To Introduce Myself...

*O*ver forty years ago, exactly one month after graduating from the University of Illinois with a BA in philosophy (try finding work in that field, Socrates), I got a job at one of Chicago's biggest ad agencies. That was a miracle of sorts, because I had no education or training in the field, but I did have a knack for getting ideas and creating ads, especially TV commercials. Maybe it was destiny. Or maybe it was in my genes. After all, my father Vincent R. Vassolo had created the Maytag Loneliest Man In Town for Leo Burnett, and enjoyed a run of almost five decades in the business as a copywriter and creative director.

I began plying my trade as a creative advertising professional on July 16, 1969, steadily rising from coffee-fetching junior copywriter to creative director, executive producer and, finally, Sr. VP, director of creative services. Over the past forty years, I've worked at the biggest and best brand-building agencies in the world, including Burnett, Y&R, FC&B, and McCann, as well as some of the smallest, most creative boutiques. I've also worked as Director of Marketing Communications in corporations, ranging from rock-solid Rockwell to "trying to make it on a wing and a prayer" e-commerce start-ups, as well as fledgling high-tech companies. And I've founded businesses, including Vim, Vigor & Vassolo LLC, an agency that specializes in creating marketing strategies, advertising and marcom that resonate with Baby Boomers.

I started thinking about marketing to Boomers during the early 1990s. That's when I worked at advertising by day, and at night I earned a master's degree in clinical gerontology followed by a post-graduate professional certificate in gerontology counseling.

I branched out from advertising, because I love unexplored territory. And there's nothing as unexplored or unknown as the vast implications of what might happen when

2

a huge group of people age way beyond normal expectations. In America, particularly, the graying population represents an unprecedented opportunity for businesses to profit from understanding and meeting the needs of the biggest, richest market segment in the history of the world: The Baby Boomers.

I'm a Boomer myself, of course, and I've always been a believer in Positive Aging, even when I was quite young. It's not an easy thing to embrace wholeheartedly, because as you age, life's challenges can run from merely irritating to quite daunting. But long ago, I learned that Positive Aging is the only way to go, because living indifferently and lethargically is a waste of breath.

My lifelong commitment to Positive Aging has paid off nicely, because it's helped me achieve a great deal despite the fact that I've had Crohn's disease for well over 50 years (I've also got 15 surgeries under my belt—literally). Through it all, I've raised a family, had a long, successful career, and in my spare time, I earned a 7th degree black belt in Kenpo karate, which I taught for over a quarter of a century.

If you're interested in self-defense, you can find my books *Kamikaze Fighting: The Self-Defense Of Last Resort* and *Desperate Measures: Unarmed Self-Defense Against*

Guns, Knives and Clubs at Amazon. They were published using my middle name, Michael, rather than Vincent. I look a bit different in the books, because during my martial arts years I had a killer perm—I called it my war bonnet.

While it's true that Crohn's disease takes a lot out of a person, if I had chosen to curl up in a fetal position and languish, I would have been reduced to a living death. My belief in Positive Aging has always kept me interested in the possibilities of tomorrow. As a consequence, I've remained as fully engaged as possible with daily life, day after day, decade after decade.

Of course, I'm far from unique. In fact, I'm just your average Boomer. And although Positive Aging may sound like some New Age mumbo jumbo, Baby Boomers like me are going to demonstrate its real meaning through living rather than lip service, no matter what ails us. Wait and see. But not too long, or you'll miss out on a lot of the upside.

Positively The Most Promising Opportunity In The History Of American Business

*T*he Baby Boomers are about to cause a seismic shift in purchasing patterns, transforming markets and creating new ones from coast to coast. They're 75 million strong, and they spend over $2 trillion dollars yearly on everything from pharmaceuticals to fashion.

Right now, the Boomers are sitting on more expendable income than any other group of consumers, and they're hitting their peak spending years.

Somehow, though, the vast majority of marketers keep overlooking them in favor of trendy teens and post-adolescent consumers. For most companies, this is a foolish oversight that's largely rooted in ageism.

If you consider yourself a savvy marketer, you can't afford to think this way and pass up the countless profit-making opportunities brought about by the blossoming of the Boomers.

But if you hope to successfully market to this quirky group, you need to go well beyond merely devising tried and true (read: boring) strategies and tactics. You need to execute advertising and integrated marcom programs that reflect values like individualism and Positive Aging to ensure that all of your communications resonate with Boomers.

And you can only do this by dispelling antiquated notions of what aging means. Instead, you must communicate with each individual Boomer one-on-one, replacing stereotypes with realistic values, attitudes, strategies, copy and visuals based on the power of Positive Aging.

Why It's Simply Smart Business
To Embrace Positive Aging

Historically, aging has been seen as a time of increasing disability and frailty inexorably leading to death, but the Boomers refuse to accept that point of view. That's why the new paradigm of Positive Aging positively resonates with them. That's also why advertising and marketing communications that mirror Positive Aging's many facets can profoundly influence Boomer buying decisions.

So, if you haven't already done it, the smart move now is to take a close look at your products and services, and ask yourself how you can reposition them toward the burgeoning Boomer market. Of course, this isn't to suggest that you walk away from your current markets. Rather, it's about adding profitable sales in ways you might never have dreamt possible.

What makes this new opportunity so lucrative is that there's a proven methodology that can help add incremental profits that will grow your bottom line. It's the Boomer Strategy Blueprint™, and it can help almost any business grow in nearly any economic climate, because it can help you apply the principles of Positive Aging to your advertising and marcom. We'll cover concepts related to Positive Aging, as well as the Boomer Strategy Blueprint later in this book.

Positive Aging Can Increase Sales
For Virtually Any Business

But before you can change your profit outlook, you have to change your mindset. In order to embrace the concept of Positive Aging, you have to transform the way you think about and relate to Boomers. It begins with banishing stereotypes, but that's just the beginning.

Your strategy and tactics have to be grounded in a genuine respect for each Boomer's individualism. Your advertising and marcom have to be brimming with concepts that conjure enthusiastic images of Positive Aging. Your writing and visual executions have to energize Boomers with messages that reflect vitality and independence. Understand and adapt to the Boomer mindset, and you can develop new markets, expanding the profit-making potential of your products and services.

If you think your products and services can't be profitably repositioned against the Boomer market, you haven't creatively searched for the opportunities that are right under your nose. The Boomer Strategy Blueprint is an innovative way to reconsider brands in a new light in order to discover incremental profit-making opportunities. It's also an engaging, exciting and valuable tool for brainstorming innovative approaches to the Boomer market.

When you compare your current approach to the Boomer Strategy Blueprint, you'll discover that it's like the difference between panning for that rare gold nugget and striking the mother-lode of increased profitable sales.

Think Like A Couselor, Sell Like An Ad Pro

To really connect with Boomers, you need to know how to reach each person as a unique individual. In a very real sense, you need to possess the depth and breadth of understanding and empathy that a counselor has.

Of course, there are many gerontology counselors who know how to communicate quite effectively with Boomers, but they don't know a thing about advertising or marketing communications. Use one of them as a consultant, and you're likely to get lots of statistics and some psychobabble, but very little practical advice you can use in selling to Boomers.

Likewise, there are lots of brilliant ad execs, including very talented writers and art directors, who can sell anything you can name, but they don't know a thing about how to communicate effectively with Boomers. To make matters worse, the vast majority of them have no desire to even try. Instead they go for what they believe to be the easy money, focusing on over-leveraged impulse buyers, even as the credit boom goes bust.

What you really need to penetrate the Boomer market are professionals who are as adept at gerontology counseling as they are at advertising and marcom. Of course, in the business world, that combination of experience and expertise is rare, indeed, but it's out there.

For instance, in the fall of 1994, an advertising creative director wrote about what he called GeroMarketing. Uninspired for an ad guy, perhaps, but better than Industrial Gerontology, which was the label suggested by one of his professors. As he developed the concept, he renamed it Creative GeroMarketing™ because it combined many of the key principles of creative advertising and marcom with those of gerontology counseling. Integrating insights and tools from both fields, he devised innovative techniques that can be used to reach what he calls the Boomer Buying Center™ where all sales begin.

Taking his pioneering effort to the next level has proven to be very exciting. Frustrating, too. But it's worth the effort, because as he's learned, thinking like a counselor and selling like an ad exec can be very rewarding.

Of course, that guy is me, and you'll learn how to use the techniques mentioned above a little later in this book.

To Reach Boomers, It Pays To Think Lke A Shrink
Or, more specifically, like a bona fide gerontology counselor. That means going beyond the conventional wisdom of conventional research about Boomers, and listening to

their needs, deeply and actively. You'll begin to genuinely appreciate how they think and feel. Then you'll be able to communicate with them in respectful, insightful ways that excite and motive them to act.

Don't Trust Anyone Under 50, Not Even Yourself

To really understand the Boomers, it's imperative that you've lived through the developmental stages they have. The fact is that the overwhelming majority of younger people simply don't have the life experience that allows them to go beyond an intellectual understanding of what the Boomers are all about. And it shows in the advertising strategies and tactics that they employ.

Strange as it may seem, this is the one area of advertising and marketing where gray hair isn't just necessary, it's indispensable. When it comes to establishing rapport with an audience, there's no substitute for active listening and insightful messaging based on shared life experiences. As many sincere marketers and advertisers have found, superficial communications simply won't fly with sophisticated consumers like the Boomers.

The most powerful advertising and marketing communication campaigns resonate with the four things

Boomers hold sacred: independence, identity, authenticity and community. In addition, you always have to keep in mind the most important values of all: individualism and Positive Aging. If you're under 50, these may never even have occurred to you.

Boomers Turn Branding Upside Down

Boomers are bright, opinionated and socially connected, so they'll decide what your brand means rather than having you or some trendsetter define it for them. As a marketer, your challenge is to craft ways that will encourage Boomers to spread the good word about your products and services to friends and neighbors. That means you've got to be a good reporter, as well as an engaging storyteller, and it doesn't hurt to have a sense of humor, as well. With the Boomers, the trite idea that the customer is always right becomes a literal truth, because, as always, they'll have it their way, thanks.

To take full advantage of what may prove to be the most promising economic opportunity in American history, you've got to genuinely understand the Boomers on many levels. To reach them, you need to be as sensitive as a counselor and as dynamic as an advertising creative director. This book will help you become a little of both.

Soon, you'll begin to discover new ways to help Boomers see your brand in a more meaningful light, and each will redefine it in their own positive way. As they do, you'll be able to see the results using the most important research instrument every devised: the cash register.

You Think Too Young

*Y*ou're in marketing or advertising. That means you're almost certainly too young to really understand how to talk to Baby Boomers.

No aspect of business is more ageist than marketing, and advertising is the worst offender of all. In fact, much of today's advertising suggests that the industry is run by sophisticated adolescents with little understanding of and no respect for effective strategy, especially when it comes to reaching history's biggest and most important market segment, the Baby Boomers.

Too much of today's advertising goes for easy laughs and

easier pop references that play right to the heart of America's youth-oriented culture. It's the worst kind of style-over-substance marketing communication, and it's going to fall from grace rather rapidly in the coming years, because the Boomers are arriving with a resounding roar.

Like it or not, as always, the Boomers will have their way. Just based on sheer numbers, they've repeatedly transformed existing markets and created new ones. Some savvy businesses have already jumped on the Boomer bandwagon. If you haven't yet, it may be because you're blinded by youth.

It's not really your fault, though. We live in a youth-worshipping culture that harbors fearful prejudices about older adults, as well as the aging process in general. But the Boomers are a decidedly different breed than your granddaddy, because they think and act much more individualistically than earlier generations of older adults. They also have lots if money, as well as the time and inclination to spend it freely.

Getting a share of that cash flow, however, can be quite challenging, because Boomers have uniquely self-centered mindsets that influence when, where, why and how they spend that money. Understanding how to relate to those mindsets on a one-to-one basis is the key to unlocking new sources of profitability you probably haven't even dreamt of yet.

Be skeptical at your own peril, because the numbers don't lie. Over the next generation, the median age of consumers will continue to increase, and the lucrative cohort of big spending Boomers will also grow. But to profit from this demographic shift, you have to understand how to talk to these highly individualistic people, and that's going to take a radical paradigm shift away from pandering to the cult of youth toward the reality of genuinely relating to older adults. It's going to be the biggest change in marketing history, and those who master communicating with and motivating Boomers to buy will profit from it the most.

To get started, you need to see your products and services in a new light, and you need to devise marketing strategies that cater to the heart of the Boomers. Perhaps, the most vexing problem is that although it's easy to quantify the Boomers, it's not easy to accurately define the group as a whole. Unlike impulsive pre-pubescent teens and trendy post-adolescent adults, Boomers are individualists. That means you can't succeed by bombarding them with superficial mass media communications. Instead, you have to actually communicate person-to-person with them as if they were thinking, feeling individuals, not just buying machines who will salivate over the latest fad or fashion.

Learning to understand, appreciate and communicate person-to-person with each individual Boomer is what this book is all about. It will give you many insights, big and small, that will help you come to understand Boomers as complex, multifaceted human beings. Once you gain this understanding, you'll be equipped to devise insightful strategies and creative communications that reach Boomers in ways that motivate them to act. And if you do it skillfully and artfully, you'll surely profit.

In case you're wondering whether I'm just another self-styled expert spouting off like some slick Huckster (check out the 1947 film), keep in mind that in addition to decades of experience in advertising and marketing communications, I'm also the father of GeroMarketing™, a term that I coined in 1994. I understand Boomers and I know how to sell to them, but I do it in a deep, even soulful way, because that's what it takes to relate to these complex consumers.

Another thing that qualifies me as an expert on Boomers is that I'm one myself. Born in 1947, I'm a Leading-Edge Boomer, so I've actually lived through the developmental stages and issues that I'll be discussing. Make no mistake, though, this isn't an academic treatise; it's a practical guide that can help you unlock the hidden profits in your business no matter what you're selling.

To get things rolling, let's get a feel for where the Baby Boomers are coming from by meeting the archetype: Benjamin Braddock who was born in 1946 and came of age in 1967 in *The Graduate*.

The Birth Of The Boom

*T*o get a little gut level insight into what the Baby Boomers are about, watch *The Graduate* again, or at least the final scenes. The end of the film offers a vivid depiction of individualism in action, and it shows just how nonrational a force it can be.

As you'll recall, Benjamin Braddock is a freshly graduated nebbish who becomes the sex object of an alluring middle-aged adulteress, Mrs. Robinson. It's not clear whether this man-child is alienated and adrift or just plain lazy, but he sure is horny. After graduating from college, his parents prod him, while he pokes his paramour. Gradually, he begins to grapple with the shifting sexual mores of the 60s, as well as his feelings of guilt and estrangement.

As the film progresses, Benjamin becomes increasing conflicted as he rebels against society's conventional customs and stifling expectations. Commitment to the "plastics" lifestyle doesn't resonate with him, so he struggles to discover what he truly wants. As his self-absorption grows more focused, his individuality begins to nudge its head out of the clouds of apathy. As a result, his post-adolescent discontent with the status quo becomes intensified and validated, at least in his own mind.

Watching this unfold is like viewing the birth of Boomer individualism, which may have developed as an easy and gratifying answer for a generation that felt confused, exploited and betrayed by The Man. Benjamin's own Coming of Age odyssey provides no hint of where it might end up. One thing is clear, however, he has discovered that he can mollify his yearnings by exercising his independence and ingenuity, two hallmarks of Boomer individualism. For much of the movie, his rebellion is mostly an internal struggle. But when he finally takes decisive action, it's a compelling example of the kind of mindset that gave birth to the Boomers.

The Graduate is a funny, fascinating flick that compares

and contrasts the values of two warring generations and ideologies. Even in 1967, it put an exclamation point on the growing dissatisfaction that budding Baby Boomers had with the status quo. That discontent grew exponentially as the Boomers turned away from the alienation bred by "things as they should be," and looked inward for new and unique ways to create meaningful lives.

Individualism became the normative value for Boomers as the horrors of the Vietnam War, assassinations and charred inner cities gave way to the hardcore cynicism born of the post-Watergate Era. For the Boomers, "Don't trust anyone over 30" ultimately morphed into what might be individualism's anthem: "Don't trust anyone but yourself."

Impulsive individualism was reflected in *The Graduate's* final, and most telling scene, when Benjamin rescues Elaine from the all-too predictable life promised by her whitebread groom. The symbolism of individuality versus conventionality is joyously portrayed as the once mousy Benjamin barges in on one of society's most solemn ceremonies and steals the bride right off the altar just as she's about to seal her fate by kissing the groom. Benjamin's passionate appeal is so convincing that she readily rejects a world that has inflicted so many unwelcome expectations on her delicate psyche.

As a last resort, Mrs. Robinson insists, "It's too late!" Elaine answers, "Not for me!" Mom counters with a couple of slaps to her impertinent daughter's chops just before the rebellious lass dashes off with her savior. In a final gesture of contempt, Benjamin uses a large gold cross—his Excalibur—to fend off their pursuers. He then uses it like a dead bolt on the church's big glass doors, locking the enemy in their own little world and out of his and Elaine's.

The newly liberated couple streaks to the nearest bus stop, two mavericks on a heady journey toward who knows where. With everyone and everything left behind, they ride off in the back of a bus, secure in the knowledge that their declaration of independence has prevailed over the forces of orthodoxy that threatened to rob them of their very souls. The other passengers silently stare at them in disbelief (a wedding grown will draw those kinds of looks in the back of a bus), as Benjamin and Elaine settle into their private reveries to *The Sounds of Silence.*

Like all good art, *The Graduate* was ahead of its time in the way it so vividly showcased the Boomers' penchant for individualism. With time, that uncompromising attitude toward the world at large has become a primary value that colors the way Boomers make decisions about everything from divorce to honeymooning to buying annuities and retirement villas.

After a torrid weekend of passion, Benjamin and Elaine probably went their separate ways, eventually settling down with someone else. But although they may have ultimately settled for a more conventional lifestyle than the finale might suggest, it's highly unlikely that they ever abandoned the belief that they're each the center of their own little universe. And, in the final analysis, living that belief is what being a Baby Boomer is all about.

Creativity Works Magic
With Boomers

*A*t the Dawn of Advertising, a sage noted, "It ain't creative, if it don't sell!" As a strategy-driven copywriter and creative director, I couldn't agree more.

In advertising and marketing communications, the bottom line is the bottom line. Period. Whether you're promoting products, services, ideas, or all three, making the sale is all that counts. All else is window dressing, because if the cash register doesn't ring, the marketing strategies and creative executions aren't worth the time, money or effort it took to create them.

Of course, that doesn't mean you can ignore creativity

24

in favor of communicating things in ways that would make even Bean Counters yawn. You've seen the kind of advertising and marcom that results from that approach. Ugh!

Remember, you can't bore Baby Boomers into buying. So, if you try to tell or sell them something using Drivel and Pablum (wasn't that a Kansas City agency that closed back in the '90s?), don't expect Boomers to greet your efforts with anything but a yawn, or worse, disdain.

And keep in mind that if creativity is magic, strategy-driven creativity that actually works is genius. To get the job done, you need to employ the most creative writers, art directors and producers around, but finding them can be as grueling as panning for gold.

I've hired and mentored many creative professionals over the past forty-some years, and the truly gifted ones are rare indeed. If you're looking for creative pros who can take your business to the next level, don't bother writing tight, logical job specs for them (unless you're forced to do so by corporate fiat), because creatives defy being boxed in by anyone or anything. Irrespective of education or experience, the one common quality I've noticed, is that their creativity never fails them. Wake them up at 3 AM, give them a tough challenge, and they'll quickly come back with a very respectable professional solution, if not something that's borderline brilliant.

Managing creatives isn't a science, but it's absolutely necessary because they tend to be so enamored of themselves and their "art" that they can go off on self-indulgent tangents that may leave you scratching your head, saying, "But it looked and sounded so cool, where did we go wrong?"

To ensure that your advertising and marcom are efficient, effective marketing tools, you need a strong, visionary leader who has a natural flair for creativity, as well as a deep belief in the power of a well-wrought strategy. This person must have the experience, expertise and guts to stand up to the most flashy and pushy creative type and insist, "What's the Big Idea?" That's the only sure way to craft advertising and marcom that's as disciplined to the sales process as it is faithful to creativity.

The creative leader also has to have the skill to deftly shepherd the idea (and it sundry executions) from creation through the various levels of management approval that threaten to emasculate it. That, in a nutshell, is what a good creative director does.

Creative directors of the future will be required to challenge their own prejudices when it comes to communicating with Boomers. Most of the hotshots in the field are just too young to understand or empathize with Boomers, and that will be their downfall.

Boomers are sophisticated, media-savvy consumers who have seen and heard it all. They simply won't tolerate advertising or marcom that tries to trick or talk down to them. And no business can afford to try to marginalize the Boomers, because there are just too many of them, and they're too affluent.

But be warned: If you get on their wrong side, Boomers can be just as temperamental as teens. The difference is that they have a lot more money, and they won't spend it as impulsively as younger, trendy consumers, so you better be spot on with the creative approaches you take, in both concept and tone.

Fortunately, Boomers are as open to creative communications as anyone else. However, they tend to be rather contemplative in their shopping and deliberate in their buying. That makes them the toughest audience out there, so you need a lot more experience and expertise to reach them.

And you're got to know more than just advertising and marcom. You've got to know the basic principles and techniques of gerontology counseling. That may sound esoteric, but as you'll see, that discipline can provide practical ways to understand, communicate with and motivate Boomers.

Reaching Boomers may well be the biggest challenge facing marketers over the next generation. If you have the skill and wisdom to devise and stick with a sound strategy, and if you have the courage to express it in the most creative ways possible, you've got a great shot at getting your share of this lucrative market. Just remember, when you're communicating with Boomers, there's nothing more compelling than a memorable message that's actually worth remembering.

The Boomer Strategy Blueprint in this book is the product of decades of advertising and marcom experience informed by clinical gerontology, a discipline that's all about meaningfully communicating with older adults. At first glance, this strategic tool may look simple, but it can be devilishly difficult to complete in a way that makes it genuinely useful. So keep reading, and you'll gain the knowledge and insights needed to use this sophisticated tool like an expert.

Along the way, you'll need to become a little more introspective. You'll find that by carefully considering your own thoughts, feelings and attitudes about aging, you'll start to understand why concepts related to Positive Aging are so important to wooing the Boomers.

Old Is The New Young

*Y*ou may think that "Old is the new young," is just a facile phrase meant to shake up your preconceived notions, and it is. Across the board, marketers have effectively ignored Boomers who have tons of money in favor of trendy teens and post-adolescents, many of whom can't find a well-paying job to support their credit card addiction.

Simple common sense dictates that marketers should turn their thinking around, yet they seem to have little or no interest in learning how to sell to all those Boomers with bulging bankrolls. Too bad, because in some ways Boomers are even more self-indulgent than their kids and grandkids, and they're eager to spend on themselves before eventually passing whatever's left to the next generation.

If you're interested in adding incremental profits to your bottom line, it's time to break the chains of your youth-worshipping marketing mentality, shed your ageist prejudices, and ponder the meaning of the Coming of the Boomers. Do that, and you'll discover how your products and services can meet their unique and varied needs and desires. Try to understand each Boomer as an individual by asking, "Who is this guy or gal anyway?" If you listen in just the right way—with your third ear—you'll discover that the answers are often related to the Power of Positive Aging. So get with it now. "Think old" and discover the hidden profits in your products and services.

The Death Of Ageism

*G*erontologist Robert Butler coined the word "ageism" in 1968, not long after the first Baby Boomers reached the age of majority. Basically, Butler defined ageism as looking at older adults in a way that strips them of their individuality. Like any pernicious –ism, it replaces uniqueness with simpleminded stereotypes that make the ageist more comfortable. It also fuels attitudes and behaviors that diminish the humanity of older adults, making them easier to ignore or abuse while marginalizing them to the edges of daily life.

Tolerance of ageism will begin to end with the advent of the Baby Boomers, a huge, rich and powerful group of individualists who won't sit still for being treated like anything less than the center of their own little universe. As they enter "old" age, they're going to mark that milestone in ways that will force us to transform how we treat older adults, and ultimately that will be good for business and society.

Of course, this transformation won't come without a struggle. However, if the history of the Boomer Movement is any indication of their power to move mountains, it will inevitably happen. They were, after all, among the leaders in overcoming the toxic effects of racism and sexism. And they'll inspire future generations to keep at it until those poisons have been completely eliminated from our society.

Historically, ageism has always been demeaning to older adults, but almost all of them have borne abuse stoically, much in the same way that women did before the feminist movement broke the shackles of America's male-dominated culture. Interestingly, Betty Friedan, author of *The Feminine Mystique* published in 1963, took on ageism when she wrote *The Fountain of Age* thirty years later. Some people just don't know their place.

If you aspire to sell anything to Boomers, you need to first thoughtfully examine, assess and rethink your attitudes about aging, because if you slip and appear to be ageist in your advertising or marcom, they'll never forgive you or your business. However, if you structure your advertising and marcom strategies and executions based on the assumption that Boomers are genuinely important individuals, you'll grow your business. The bottom line is that when you marginalize Boomers, you marginalize your profit potential.

Young or old, we're all ageist to some extent. There's not a person among us who doesn't knowingly or unknowingly have at least a handful of ageist tendencies. That's why as a thought leader in business, you need to discover and stay in touch with your thinking, feelings, attitudes and behaviors concerning older adults. Here are a dozen thought starters to help you begin what will be a very profitable process personally, as well as professionally.

1. *Do you believe that you're an ageist?*

    If you take umbrage at the very suggestion, perhaps you protest a bit too much. Take a closer look at your most cherished and certain beliefs about aging, and see if there's any prejudice to be found.

2. *Are you afraid of aging?*

    It's a natural fear, particularly in our youth-worshipping

culture. But if you don't face down that fear, you're setting yourself up for a horrendous fall if you're lucky enough to grow old one day. In the meantime, your fear will color your advertising and marcom decisions, much to your company's detriment.

3. *Have you made an effort to learn about key aspects of aging?*

The more realistically informed you are about aging and what to expect, the better you'll be able to evaluate and resist the inaccurate and negative stereotypes so often associated with the aging process. Strive to understand the differences between what's relevant in aging and what isn't, and you'll be on the path to enlightenment.

4. *Do you harbor misinformation and erroneous beliefs about aging?*

Once you understand the important aspects of aging, do you use facts to actively challenge the misconceptions and myths that can distort your thinking and behavior? Be sure to analyze your "positive" prejudices as well as your negative ones.

5. *Do you believe in the stereotypes of aging?*

   To begin to answer this, examine the language you use when talking about aging, then go from there.

6. *Do you appreciate the difference between ageism and discrimination?*

   You may never have done a single discriminatory thing to any older adult, yet still be an ageist at heart. In fact, some very well-meaning people overcompensate and treat elders with so much deference that it actually becomes an embarrassment. Better to stick with a straightforward, realistic, person-to-person approach that doesn't discriminate based on the age of the people involved.

7. *Have you carefully listened to how ageism can affect Boomers?*

   You can do this informally by speaking with them one on one, or you can do it more formally in a series of focus groups. Whatever you choose, there's no substitute for going directly to the source.

8. *Have you monitored advertising, marcom and the media, observing how they reflect aspects of aging and ageism?*

Carefully considering the negative ways in which older adults are portrayed in marcom, ads, commercials, films and television is crucial to understanding and overcoming ageism.

9. *Have you considered advocating against ageism?*
Obviously, sponsoring an initiative that champions the fight against ageism can do wonders for your company's image. But on a personal level, when someone you know uses ageist language or images, do you tactfully advise them to reconsider their attitude? Face it, even innocent jokes help keep ageism alive.

10. *Are you careful about your own language and behavior toward older adults?*
No matter how loving and generous you may be, nobody's perfect. A little self-examination just might prove profitable.

11. *Do you talk openly about aging issues and ageism with your staff?*
Hidden ageism that's never spoken about can be even more destructive than the overt kind, because it makes it

easier for people to wallow in ignorance. A powerful way to fight ageism is to showcase people who don't fit any stereotypes in your advertising and marcom.

12. *Can you build intergenerational bridges to promote better mutual understanding?*
Ageism thrives in the Petri dish of ignorance. However, when all generations understand that they're interconnected throughout their lifespan, they'll begin to appreciate the power they have to affect each others' well-being. Over time, this will reduce negative attitudes against young and old, alike.

An exercise like the one above may not be very appealing or comfortable, but it can be invaluable for your business and yourself. Understanding ageism may seem like an odd subject for a book about advertising to Boomers, but it's actually crucial. Eliminating ageism is one of the keys to successfully communicating with them because it will help enable what every Boomer strives for: Positive Aging.

The Power Of
Positive Aging

The Elusive Meaning Of Positive Aging.

*T*he precise meaning of Positive Aging is impossible to pin down because there are as many different definitions as there are people. Although it's true that research can provide valuable insights into the meaning of the concept, current findings can't be synthesized into a meaningful whole that truly gets to the heart of the matter.

The reason is that, ultimately, the most important definition is the one that each individual believes on a gut level. That definition, no matter how simple or complex, no matter how factually accurate or inaccurate, will form the foundation for the belief system that will be the guiding light for each individual's aging process. If that belief system holistically facilitates the physical, psychosocial and spiritual well-being of the individual, then it is the essence of Positive Aging, at least for that particular person.

You Have Only A Moment To Live

It's a fact. You have just a single moment to live...and then another...and then another. That's one of the keys to understanding Positive Aging. True, pondering the past and future can sometimes bring pleasure (or pain), but the fact is that everything always happens right here, right now. And the moment you recognize that fact, the moment is gone. Successful Positive Agers have learned how to live in the moment. Moment after moment after moment. This doesn't make them impulsive. On the contrary, it makes them more calmly observant—better able to contemplate what they really want. Ultimately, that has important implications for anyone who hopes to sell them anything.

How To Recognize Reality

Living in the present moment requires that you experience the immediate reality that's right under your nose. Any striving to create that reality is vain and, ultimately, self-defeating. The need to live in the present moment sounds obvious because it is, but that doesn't mean it's easy.

For a taste of living right here, right now, try this. Find a comfortable place where you can sit undisturbed for five full minutes. Then, simply watch your breath going in and out. Follow it as it gently flows in your nose and then out of your mouth. When your mind wanders, don't fret, simply bring your attention back to your breathing. It sounds simple, but it can be hard to do. However, establishing this kind of practice is extremely valuable, because it's the best way to begin to recognize reality as it unfolds moment to moment, unencumbered by the noise of thinking. Eventually, you'll come to treasure each instant—that present moment where we must all live, all of the time.

What's Reality Got to Do With Positive Aging?

It may seem odd to ask about the nature of reality in everyday life, but it's worth contemplating, if only because we so infrequently attempt to tease out the genuine facts from the fictions created by our magpie minds.

The best way to learn how to do this consistently is to expand on the exercise mentioned in the previous section.

Sit quietly and follow your breathing, gently bringing your attention back to it when your mind inevitably wanders. This practice has been around for millennia, and if you can work up to 20 or 30 minutes a day, you'll discover the rewards are more than worth the time invested.

Mindful meditation is well-known as a stress management technique, but it's so much more than that. It's actually the simplest, surest way to get in touch with and stay in touch with objective reality, from moment to moment. What's that got to do with Positive Aging? Everything, because you can't begin to wrap your mind and body around something as elusive as Positive Aging, unless and until you become adept at living in the present moment. Once you do that, you can begin to lead your life fully awake to the possibilities of the moment, and that's the essence of Positive Aging.

Staying In Touch With The Present Moment Is Tough

Living in the present moment may seem more than difficult, it may seem impossible. But before you give up on even trying, consider the alternatives. You can dwell in the past, reliving the good and brooding about the bad, but ultimately both of those outcomes are dead ends. Chronically living in the future is even worse, because it's doomed to be a concoction of fantasies about good and bad things that might happen, but seldom do. More dead ends.

Being in the moment, on the other hand, allows you to partake of reality as it actually is. It may not always be pleasant, but it's more rewarding than wasting the here and now on distorted thinking about what was or might be.

Staying in touch with the moment is the key to escaping the prison of letting life just "happen" to you. It helps you silence the incessant chatter of thinking and plumb the depths of what actually is. The more you can accurately perceive reality, the more you can maximize the possibility that you'll make the most of your life at any given moment. And that's what Positive Aging is all about, no matter how you define it.

How Do You Define Positive Aging?

The way you define Positive Aging becomes crucial as you grow older, because if you don't think for yourself, you'll end up accepting stereotypes that will erode your sense of well-being. To begin to define Positive Aging for yourself, you must clearly identify and then stay in touch with how you feel about various aspects of aging. The ageism exercise in the last chapter can help with that.

Here's another exercise that will help you come to terms

with the way you think about aging. It will also help you redefine and refine the way you age. Start by making a written list of five negative beliefs you have about aging and five positive ones. How realistic are those beliefs? Which have the greatest influence on the quality of your life and the way you act? Which strengthen your sense of well-being? Which diminish it? Do your beliefs indicate that you buy into cultural stereotypes about aging, or do you clearly think things through for yourself? Do you feel your beliefs are set in stone, or can they be modified?

Finally, pick the single most significant negative belief that you have about aging, and ask yourself how you can overcome it. Then pick the single most positive—and accurate—belief, and ask yourself how you can use it as a building block for growth. This is the trailhead of the path toward Positive Aging.

What You Think About Aging Is Crucial

Fact is, what you think about anything is of great importance, because to a significant degree, what you think largely determines your life experience. The idea that you are what you think has been around for millennia. Almost two thousand years ago, Marcus Aurelius wrote, "A man's life is what his thoughts make of it." More recently, Ralph Waldo Emerson said, "A man is what he thinks about all day long." Seems obvious, yet how often do you really think about what you think?

It's an important question, because the difference between seeing various aspects of aging in a positive versus a negative light can be like the difference between heaven and hell. Of course, there are certainly lots of very potentially troubling things that can come with aging, from physical to psychosocial challenges. That's why reframing negative perceptions in a constructive way is a key ingredient in Positive Aging. Reframing teaches you that you can control how you think about reality—that you can see negatives more positively or even eliminate them altogether.

Of course, reframing doesn't happen by accident. It takes consistent effort, but it's worth it when you consider the enhanced quality of life it can bring. If you're unconvinced, compare your models for positive and negative aging. Do they seem happy and fulfilled or cranky and frustrated? What is it about their lives that makes them that way? Does it have anything to do with the way they perceive reality?

The bottom line question is: What will you choose for yourself? Will you actively embrace the ways of Positive

Aging or drift into a negative way of life? One thing is certain: The choices you make about what you think will color your days, no matter what your age.

Why Positive Aging Resonates With Baby Boomers

Boomers embrace Positive Aging because the idea that all good things are possible—indeed, inevitable—for them has been virtually programmed into their psychosocial DNA. People who don't understand Boomers see them as extremely self-centered, but they also tend to be more altruistic than previous generations. That can have important implications for marketers who target them.

For insight into why Boomers seem so self-centered, Google psychologist Carl Rogers and unconditional positive regard. Humanist psychologists like Rogers believed that unconditional acceptance of the individual would provide optimal conditions for personal growth. During the Boomers' formative years, the concept of unconditional positive regard was promoted in child-rearing and education, becoming a guiding light for their parents and teachers.

Unconditional positive regard holds that everyone has the innate ability to improve without changing who they actually are. Although it's true that unconditional positive regard and acceptance can lead to unadulterated selfishness, simply being self-centered isn't as negative as it sounds. In fact, it can be quite beneficial when it empowers a person to nurture self-esteem and optimism. That alone can be a driving force that energizes focused actions which enhance the individual's well-being. And that's one of the reasons why so many Boomers strive for Positive Aging.

What Positive-Aging Boomers Believe

Positive Agers know that there is an important difference between growing as you become older and simply growing older. They know that successful Positive Aging isn't about adding years to your life; it's about personal growth and making the most of what life offers under any and all circumstances.

Positive Agers also know that it's not about dodging every bullet, because that's impossible. Rather, it's about avoiding frailty by cultivating a healthful lifestyle that enhances physical, mental, social and spiritual well-being.

Cultivating various aspects of Positive Aging prepares them to meet the inevitable challenges that come with everyday life—challenges that seem to increase over time. They know that wear and tear can't be completely defeated, but becoming worn and torn can be. Positive Agers know how to face infirmity with flexibility. They know that the facts of physical aging dictate that their sense of well-being must lie beyond the limits of their bodies, even as they struggle to live within them.

"Old age ain't no place for sissies," according to a quote from Bette Davis. It rings true, because there's simply no substitute for courage in creating a positive lifestyle. But you need more than that. To be a Positive Ager, you need a sensible strategy and effective tactics to develop and maintain optimism, hope and perseverance. In the final analysis, Positive Agers believe that struggling to grow as each year passes is vastly preferable to simply growing older.

Why Positive Aging And Ageism Are Poles Apart

If you're white, you'll never be black. If you're male, you'll never be female. But no matter what your age, with luck, some day you'll be old. That's why ageism is the most self-destructive form of prejudice.

This isn't to imply that other forms of prejudice aren't destructive; it's simply the recognition that ageism is unique because it has the potential to victimize every living person. The undeniable fact that each person must grow old is what

48

makes ageism the most self-hating form of prejudice possible. Ageism is diametrically opposed to Positive Aging, because it's impossible to live constructively while courting what is essentially self-loathing. If you hate aging, on some level you hate your own life. That's a fact.

Fear and ignorance form the foundation of all prejudice, and ageism is no exception, because people who indulge in ageism project their fears of aging on older adults. They're afraid of growing old, because it seems to be filled with land mines. Positive Agers understand that although they will certainly face countless challenges, the life skills they've developed give them the ability to live a fulfilling life under any circumstances. Because they've developed the resources to cope, they have the courage to live life to the fullest. To them, age becomes just another number that they seldom even think about.

So if you want to understand Baby Boomers, you must take an honest look at yourself and root out ageism in all its manifestations. Unlike other things you fear, you can't segregate yourself from aging. You have to deal with it, because it will most certainly deal with you.

The Boomers have lived through the volatile, turbulent '60s, when the struggle for racial equality was at its most passionate. They know the destructive power of prejudice, and they're showing signs that they simply won't tolerate ageism. In fact, the next Civil Rights movement may well address ageism in all its forms, and Boomers will lead the way, because they are, after all, revolutionaries at heart.

Affluent Baby Boomers Are A Market Segment Of One
The key to reaching the Baby Boomers lies in knowing how to talk to them with psychosocial insight and sensitivity. The most affluent Boomers are Positive Agers who are worldly, well-educated and discerning. They're also self-centered, self-directed and more than a little vain. That's why effectively communicating with them often requires intelligent, plausible reframing of issues that sometimes have negative connotations, and that can be very tricky.

Research can help in understanding the Boomers, but in their hearts and souls they defy categorization, so it's best to consider them A Market Segment Of One. A glance at their history shows that they're diehard individualists who make buying decisions on their own terms not someone else's—least of all some faceless corporation that's urging them to buy, buy, buy!

This Market-Segment-Of-One concept may seem difficult to grasp at first, but it really just refers to communicating with Boomers in ways that make each feel that they're the only person in the world that really matters.

If you're a marketer who understands that and learns how to woo this demanding group of consumers, then you'll act accordingly and prosper. Chances are, though, you're going to need wise counsel to motivate the Boomers to buy, because when it comes to advertising and marcom, they've seen and heard it all.

If you want a share of the Boomer market, it pays to be versed in gerontology counseling, as well as advertising and marketing communications. Understanding the principles and techniques of gerontology counseling can help you talk about the issues of aging sensitively, realistically and with a positive tone. It also helps if you have more than a few gray hairs, because living the life of a Boomer provides a depth of realistic experience that can't be matched by mere theory.

Truly understanding Boomers and treating them like A Market Segment Of One will enable you to communicate with them in meaningful ways that resonate on levels where emotional decisions are made and motivation is born. Reach Boomers where they live, and they'll carefully consider what you have to say and what you're selling. And, if you're really skillful, you can motivate them to buy.

Boomers Bask In Reflected Images Of Positive Aging

You can't successfully market to Baby Boomers until you understand, embrace and communicate Positive Aging in a creative and deeply respectful way. To do that, you have to change the way you think about and relate to Boomers. It begins with banishing ageism and disregarding stereotypes, but that's not enough. Your writing and visual executions have to energize Boomers with messages that reflect the hallmarks of Positive Aging, like vitality, independence and commitment. Understand and appreciate the Boomer mindset, and you can develop new markets, expanding the profit-making potential of your brands and business.

To accomplish this, though, you can't just focus on market segments. Instead, understand, embrace and celebrate each person's uniqueness, because that's the key to reaching Boomers where they make their buying decisions.

Of course, speaking to Boomers with authentic, value-based communications is just part of what it takes to reflect various aspects of Positive Aging. These people are highly individualistic, so you will have to take a Boomer-Centered Approach that allows you to address each and every prospect in your target market in a genuinely personal way. This will take some serious rethinking and repositioning of what you have to offer, but it will be well worth the effort.

If you think your products and services can't be profitably repositioned against the Baby Boomer market, you haven't effectively searched for the opportunities that are right under your nose. If that's the case, you need to do a brand audit, carefully looking at what you have to offer until you create a position that strikes the mother lode with Boomers. Think of it as panning for gold—a way to help you discover the hidden profit potential that can help grow your bottom line.

Of course, once you've devised the ideal Boomer position for your product or service, you then have to find a way to carve out a niche of awareness in that all-important place called The Boomer Buying Center. What's that, you ask? Keep reading.

The Boomer Buying Center, Where Sales Are Born

A buying center is an evaluation unit whose members are responsible for assessing and making major purchasing decisions. In this book, The Boomer Buying Center is a construct which attempts to make sense of and integrate the disparate spheres of feeling, thinking, being and doing that affect the way an individual Boomer makes buying decisions. Grasp that concept, and you'll be much more likely to influence the purchases made by the most affluent, individualistic market segment in history: The Baby Boomers.

There are two key questions you need to answer: How do I gain entry to the Boomer Buying Center, and what do I do when I get there? Taking a conventional approach won't often be very effective with this decidedly unconventional group. Instead, you have to take a genuinely thoughtful, individualistic approach. You have to know how to reach each Boomer in all of his or her uniqueness. You have to put the zing in the strings of their hearts and speak to their souls with authentic insight and genuine understanding. To accomplish all this, you need to have the sensitivity and training of a skilled gerontology counselor and the experience and expertise of a top-flight conceptual creative director.

If that sounds simple enough, then you obviously get it. You're also in a tiny minority, because the vast majority of marketers and advertisers don't fully appreciate the fact that Boomers think and act in an almost timeless way, because they tend to disregard their chronological age. And they're going to continue down that path till the day they die. That's why the best approach is one that stresses positive aspects of aging, even if they sometimes seem to be more fanciful than factual. Be that as it may, Boomers simply aren't gong to settle for being old in the conventional sense, so they're never likely to act their age.

Another thing to keep in mind is that Boomers exist in infinite shades of gray. Ironically, this heterogeneous bunch which embraces individualism celebrates it in others, as well.

That's one of the chief reasons the Boomer Buying Center can be so tough to fathom.

Each Boomer's psyche consists of a jumble of thoughts, emotions, judgments, psychosocial experiences and instinctual impulses that inform purchasing decisions. But although these factors are unique for each person, there are two key values that all Boomers embrace: individualism and Positive Aging.

Individualism and Positive Aging are inextricably interwoven in Boomers because of Carl Rogers, the humanistic psychologist who created person-centered therapy in the 1950s. As the name suggests, this paradigm promotes feelings and behaviors that are decidedly self-centered and extraordinarily optimistic. One of the theory's central tenets is unconditional positive regard, which encourages accepting a person without any negative judgments of basic worth.

Boomers were raised in homes and educational environments that tended to promote this ideal, which is why they have an insatiable appetite for freedom of self-expression and fulfillment. And Boomers have had it their way for so long that they believe in the real possibility of Positive Aging. After all, they've been pampered by family and society for most of their lives, so why should the aging process deprive them of their privileged status?

When it comes to purchasing behavior, Boomers are usually nonrational and often irrational, about what they buy. This isn't surprising considering that research suggests that our brains are wired for emotional rather than logical decision-making. That's why the vast majority of purchases are driven by impulses, then rationalized with "good reasons" after the fact. It's important to keep that in mind when creating marketing strategies, advertising and marcom directed at Boomers.

Of course, that's not as easy as it seems. As facts, thoughts, emotions, judgments, opinions and impulses converge, it can look like a rush hour traffic jam. So how do you make sense of each individual's unique version of the Boomer Buying Center? The best way is to apply insights and techniques from gerontology counseling to your marketing strategy and creative executions.

As you come to understand the highly volatile dynamics inherent in the Boomer Buying Center, you can accelerate and direct buying decisions in ways that can increase sales of your products and services. Validate each Boomer's quest for a more fulfilling life today, and you'll profit tomorrow.

Reaching The Boomer Buying Center

*W*hen selling to Boomers, values play a crucial role because they inform the decision-making process in The Boomer Buying Center. The two key Boomer values are individualism and Positive Aging. Individualism inspires the quest for aging well, and Positive Aging is made up of everything that's required to help Boomers succeed in that pursuit, including their unique hopes, dreams and aspirations.

As Boomers increasingly strive for Positive Aging, their values will continue to shift from materialistic to meaningful. With each passing year, Boomers will become more contemplative about every facet of their lives. As that happens, their reasons for buying will become more than skin deep. As a consequence, motivating them to purchase will take more than trendy techniques aimed at increasing impulse purchases. Selling them will require genuinely meaningful communication based on insight into what motivates them to act.

This trend is already becoming apparent. With each passing year, the Boomers have grown increasingly thoughtful when it comes to making buying decisions. And as a result of recent adverse economic developments, they've made a virtue out of value shopping, living more frugally while seeking out chic on the cheap. That means in order to penetrate the Boomer Buying Center, you must find ways to fulfill the needs and wants of a generation that is used to being catered to but is now on a budget.

Once profligate spenders, many Boomers are no longer trying to keep up with their neighbors so much as outwit them. Although it may be true that many Boomers aren't particularly well-prepared for high living in the future, they still love to spend. And they'll continue to seek luxury, but on their terms. To succeed, you must make them feel like they've outsmarted not only their own personal circumstances but also The System that has put a dent in their retirement plans.

Marketers who don't understand and respect Boomer values risk making them feel marginalized, and that's a recipe for disaster. Research can help identify and clarify values, but addressing them in sensitive ways that resonate in the Boomer Buying Center takes a unique skill set which encompasses advertising and marcom, as well as gerontology counseling.

Why gerontology counseling? Because in order to engage and motivate Boomers, you have to precisely identify and communicate with the issues that go to the heart of the matter—their Buying Center—where they ultimately make their purchasing decisions. However, the journey to that special place, where reason and emotion converge in a jumble, is complex and confusing, so you need the training and insight of a counselor who knows how to understand and empathize with Boomers. Then, when you reach their Buying Center, you have to communicate in a way that motivates them to take action. That's where advertising and marcom expertise come into play.

Exactly What Is A Baby Boomer Value?

That's a challenging question, because Boomer values are as diverse as the individuals themselves. It's tempting to succumb to the easy answers provided by current research, but trying to neatly categorize an iconoclastic group like the Boomers can lead to dead ends that waste time, effort and marketing dollars.

If the Boomers have anything in common, it's a deep distrust of authoritarianism. This mistrust is justified given the political and social turmoil of the 1960s, when America's biggest cities burned, beloved leaders were gunned down, and the war in Vietnam raged on. As a result, the relative tranquility of the 1950s quickly gave way to a divided country that was part battleground, part cauldron of change.

The Boomers questioned the most sacred societal values, and the sentiment behind the slogan "Never trust anyone over 30" at times morphed into "Never trust anyone. Period." Shaken loose from mainstream moorings, each Boomer was left to create a unique path in life. This led to a form of individualism that's often been mistaken for total selfishness when it's really more like very active autonomy.

Deep-seated individualism makes Boomers hard to pin down in terms of values, and typical research isn't always helpful in focusing the dialogue between marketer and Boomer.

A quick Google reveals that commoditized research

includes the following as Boomer values: Good health, fitness, functionality, well-being, close relationships with family and friends, altruism, kindness, compassion, self-respect, spirituality, intellectual curiosity, fun, happiness, financial security, power, recognition, excitement, balance, civility, conservatism and liberalism. Really narrows it down, doesn't it? Imagine trying to speak one on one with a Boomer using those kinds of research findings as a guiding light for your advertising and marcom.

Individualism, The Boomers' Core Value

Although much has been written about the relevance of Boomer values to marketing, it's still virtually impossible to predict the buying behavior of so large and diverse a group. The reason for this is that individualism is the Boomers' most stable, long-term value. As such, it also serves as the guiding light for the buying decisions they make.

Of course, many other values can play a key supporting role in influencing Boomer buying behavior, but those values revolve in constellations around the core of individualism, radiating out from the most to least important. That means when it comes to how, why, when, where and what they buy, Boomers will have things their way, regardless of what the rest of the world may think.

Rooted in the '60s, Boomer individualism transcended the traditional standards that limited the way previous generations thought and acted. As a result, Boomers tend to place their goals and desires over those of the community or nation.

And they won't tolerate being manipulated or meddled with when making decisions. Trying to dictate to them is worse than futile, because it can lead to a perceived lack of respect, which can result in the worst kind of word-of-mouth advertising imaginable. Diss the Boomers, and they'll let the whole world know.

So as you navigate the rugged terrain of reason and emotion that leads to the Boomer Buying Center, keep in mind that road is paved with individualism. Also remember two other things. First, reason may help Boomers rationalize and validate the "Why" of buying in their minds, but emotion begins the decision-making process at gut level. Second, while individualism and other values may lead the way to the Buying Center, it takes the finesse of a counselor with advertising and marcom experience and expertise to open the door.

Speak Directly to Baby Boomer Values,
And You'll Be Heard

Although the most important Boomer values are individualism and Positive Aging, it helps to consider a handful of other values, most of which are derived from gerontology counseling rather than consumer research.

PERSONAL SIGNIFICANCE…every Boomer feels that he or she is capable of making a real difference in this world, and you've got to convince them that you believe the very same thing. Once you've accomplished that, you then need to show them how your product or service will help them make their mark.

EXCELLENCE…Boomers are intelligent, well-informed and picky about what they buy. They know quality when they see, and they're more than willing to pay a premium for it. That's why you've got to convince them that you can deliver the best possible products and services at a price that's a genuine value.

INNER STRENGTH…Boomers know who they are and what they're about, and this self-knowledge helps them make their own choices with confidence. Your communications have to convince them that you celebrate their empowerment by treating them with genuine respect rather than facile lip service.

RESPECT…Boomers simply won't tolerate feeling marginalized. Not only have they accomplished a great deal in their lives, but they also have big plans. You've got to convince them that you understand that they want more out of life than simply a comfortable rocking chair on life's back porch.

EMPATHY…Boomers may be very self-centered, but they also care about others, often very deeply. To connect on a meaningful level, you must convince them that you share their care.

SUBSTANCE WITH STYLE…you can't fool Boomers with flashy fads like you can most younger consumers, but that doesn't mean they don't appreciate style. They do. But it has to have real substance behind it.

OPTIMAL HEALTH AND WELLNESS…Boomers don't expect to die young or unwell, for that matter. They expect to live a vigorous life, brimming with energy and enthusiasm right up to the very end. And they need you to share that expectation and help show them the way.

AUTHENTICITY…living through the '60s and beyond has made Boomers crave electrifying experiences that make them feel fully alive and connected to others, as well as their deepest roots. Their search for authenticity is inextricably interwoven with their search for meaning and happiness. Learn to tap into these primal values, and you'll be communicating with their very souls.

Things To Consider On Your Journey
To The Boomer Buying Center

Here are three key things you need to be familiar with before attempting to tap into the Boomer Buying Center. Let them really soak in, and you'll find they'll help jump-start brainstorming sessions that spark innovative advertising and marcom strategies and tactics.

MOTIVATIONAL INTERVIEWING…This counseling paradigm is ideal for conceptualizing advertising and marketing communication campaigns. It's all about moving Boomers from being totally unaware through ambivalence toward positive action. Choose and use the most appropriate techniques from this paradigm when marketing your products and services, and you'll help Boomers motivate themselves to buy your brands.

REFRAMING...This is a fundamental technique of motivational interviewing, as well as other counseling paradigms, and it can help change the way that Boomers see your products and services. Reframing helps replace the repellent prejudice born of ageism with new, uplifting concepts based firmly on various aspects of Positive Aging. It's not easy, but if you can develop strategies and tactics that redefine concepts (especially those commonly considered negative) in new ways that resonate with and excite Boomers, you can begin to motivate them to seriously consider whatever you're selling.

TAKE A HOLISTIC APPROACH...Boomers are very well educated, thoughtful and sensitive people who see themselves as multidimensional, integrated individuals, and that's exactly how you should look at them, too. Assess your products and services in terms of how they might appeal to Boomers in a holistic way, taking into account the totality of their physical, mental, psychological, social and spiritual dimensions. You also need to keep in mind that all the while you're communicating with A Market Segment Of One.

What's A Market Segment Of One?

The expression "A Market Segment Of One" might sound like mumbo jumbo, but it's an easy, reliable way to remember that although Baby Boomers may share common values, the most important is individualism. Given their experiences during the '60s, typical Boomer values revolve around a strong ego that stresses independence and self-reliance. Honor their robust sense of self by speaking meaningfully with each individual Boomer, and you'll have a good chance of moving that person from apathy to action.

A major mistake that many traditional marketers make is clustering Boomers together in convenient market segments that only superficially recognize their individuality. Herding Boomers like that might provide a loose sense of what they're like as a group, but it won't necessarily facilitate connecting with each person's unique Buying Center. A better approach is to understand, embrace and celebrate each Boomer's uniqueness.

So get inside the individual's head. Share that person's thoughts and feelings in an intimate way. Use authentic words and images that resonate with and engage that person on intellectual and emotional levels. Do all that, and you'll begin to understand what it means to address Boomers as A Market Segment Of One.

Of course, trying to precisely define this concept is as tough as trying to pin down each individual Boomer's notion of Positive Aging. It's certainly not easy, but it's not impossible. And learning how to do it is the key to unlocking the hidden profit potential in your products and services.

To turn Boomers into buyers, you need to embrace and reflect not only their values but their hopes, dreams and aspirations, as well. Do that and more in your advertising and marketing communications, and you'll reach the Boomer Buying Center where all sales begin.

The Ideal Boomer

The Trouble With Research

*C*haracterizing target markets is older than advertising. Way older. The first successful cave-to-cave salesman had an instinct for sizing up potential customers like Ms.Og before she ever rolled back her front boulder for him. He did this by drawing on what he knew about human nature and creatively applying it on an individual basis, person to person. That might seem primitive, but it's still the most effective way to reach human beings.

Trouble is, business loves numbers, because quantification seems to make slippery subjects easier to grasp, and there's some truth to that. However, the numbers game is too often used as a shield rather than a creative tool. Insecure marketers turn to numbers to justify decisions in the event things don't go exactly as planned. After all, it's a lot easier to hide behind a phalanx of figures than take the brunt of the blame for a blown call.

Of course, market research has come a long way since the dawn of selling. Today, it's a quasi-science that can drown a well-meaning marketer in minutia. Ask any research guru to describe a key market segment, and you'll get an encyclopedic recounting of facts and figures, with the kitchen sink thrown in. It may be comprehensive, but it's not lifelike. And lifeless stats make for lifeless messaging in advertising and marcom, two disciplines that thrive on intuitive creativity.

Collecting data has always been the easiest part of market research. It's knowing what to do with the raw numbers and tenuous conclusions that really counts. From the looks of most of the ads and marcom currently being spoon-fed to Baby Boomers, few marketers know how to separate useless factoids from meaningful ideas. Obvious research conclusions lead to obvious messaging, which leads to boredom, and you can't bore Boomers into buying.

I recall a very expensive, and time-consuming study that

once revealed that people wanted a lawnmower that lets them cut their grass quickly and easily. Imagine that. After wading through pages of pap, that was the bottom line conclusion! The creative group I headed up at the time didn't find that insight very informative or inspiring, but at least we had a lot less time to get the commercials done and on the air.

So, next time you're faced with a solid block of research, make like Michelangelo and chisel away everything that doesn't look like David. That takes real creativity, but if you can do it, you can be sure that you won't weigh down your creative executions with stuff that doesn't engage and resonate with your target market.

I've been in this business for over four decades, so I know that research can be valuable in fashioning a rough caricature of the Boomers, but if you want to reach their Buying Center consistently, you'll have to ferret out the things that really matter. Then you'll have to speak to each Boomer's individuality with insight and imagination, framing your messaging in ways that reaches them where they really live.

If you can do that clearly, concisely, creatively and cogently, you'll succeed. If you can't, all the facts and figures in the world won't help a bit.

Connecting With Your Ideal Boomer

The best way to create effective advertising and marcom for the Baby Boomer market is to imagine that you're speaking person to person with each individual. To do that, it helps to have a sense of whom the Ideal Boomer for your product or service might be. After all, the best way to appeal to the needs and desires that drive Boomer buying behavior is to see things through their eyes.

The first step in characterizing your Ideal Boomer is to focus on creative concepts drawn from reliable research, as well as intuition and imagination. Of course, facts and figures aren't flesh and bone, so you'll need to make a leap of faith if you're going to understand and reach that Market Segment Of One known as the Baby Boomer. In short, you need an instinctive knowledge of human nature and lots of energetic creativity to get Boomers as excited about whatever you're selling as you are.

If you're not comfortable taking leaps of faith and trusting creativity, keep in mind that the world's most innovative business leaders do exactly that, especially when the stakes are sky high. One of my favorite examples was recounted in a *BusinessWeek* article about PepsiCo America's CEO, Massimo d'Amore. (Blowing Up Pepsi, April 27, 2009).

Before Pepsi began redesigning the packaging for its flagship brand, one of the company's top branding guys, Frank Cooper III stated, "We're done being all things to all people. We are going to reach out to one very special demographic, the real you. The demographic of people who march to the beat of their own drum..." Hm-m-m, sounds like he could be talking about the Boomers.

The article didn't explain how Pepsi was going to figure out exactly who "the real you" is. They'll probably use some research to validate their creative hunches after they've executed the new packaging. That's often the way it happens, although few care to bluntly admit it. But the fact is that every marketer who aspires to do breakthrough communications has to depend on creativity to cut through the swamp of tiresome executions that pollute the media.

And that creativity has to be meaningful, too. That's why key facts from research make a good starting pointing, but if those facts aren't brought to life with an inspired creative touch, they'll be like millstones around the necks of the creative executions. And executions that don't immediately sink in, quickly sink to the bottom of the turbulent sea of media that permeates our world.

So, do your best to tightly define and characterize your

Ideal Boomer, but keep in mind that your rough caricature is only a launching pad for the creative process. Ultimately, your success will depend on how effectively and creatively you can convince Boomers that your products and services will help them validate and celebrate their individuality. Do that, and your advertising and marcom will resonate like the real thing, reaching what Pepsi might call "the real you" inside each Boomer.

Four Ways To Woo Your Ideal Boomer

Being a true individualist, the Ideal Boomer seeks to have every need, want, desire and whim catered to in a way that provides genuine value and personalized service. Of course, any consumer would love to be treated so royally. The thing about the Boomers, though, is that they insist on being courted like kings and queens. The reason for this is simple: They have a deep-rooted belief that they're special—that they are The Entitled Generation.

This attitude is unique in history, at least for so large a group. The generation before the Boomers was tempered by the Great Depression and WWII, so they've been content to make due with whatever comes their way. Following generations are learning to do the same, because they believe that once the Boomers wring all the dollars out of Social Security, Medicare and other middle class entitlement programs, there will be little left for them. Perhaps they're right.

The Boomers may have become disillusioned during the '60s, but they've never lost that feeling of entitlement. That's why they're among the world's most demanding consumers. Their motto could be: "We'll have it our way or no way at all, because we're entitled." In short, if you don't live up to their high expectations, they'll find somebody else who will.

It's not easy to transform hard-to-please Boomers into loyal customers, but it can be very rewarding. Following are four ways you can begin to woo your Ideal Boomer.

Customize Your Product's Image
For Greater Boomer Appeal

If you assume that Boomers will automatically buy whatever you're selling, prepare to go broke. The fact is that you have to do whatever it takes to make your product as appealing as possible to them. That doesn't mean rebuilding your product from the ground up, but you do have to reposition it in a way that focuses on the Boomers' needs, desires and fantasies.

For example, let's say you're selling tons of iPods to kids, and you want to grow your bottom line by 10%. A dedicated communication campaign directed to the heart of the Boomers' special interests (stressing life-enriching podcasts over pure entertainment, for instance) might well garner incremental profits without much heavy lifting. The point is that if your product's benefits and image fit The Boomer lifestyle, you've got a good shot at making a sale.

Shower Boomers With
Person-To-Person Communications

This doesn't mean merely putting each person's actual name on a mailing label. It means speaking directly to what each individual Boomer actually needs and wants. So, do your homework, then use your empathic skills and speak to them as if they were each A Market Segment Of One. Then you'll have a much clearer path to the Boomer Buying Center.

Personalize Your Service

Even if you sell something as mundane as paperclips, you're in a customer service business, so act accordingly. Whether it's at the retail level or by phone or email, make sure that your service is fast, friendly and attentive, as well as cheerfully responsive and respectful.

Right now, Apple provides stellar customer service at every point of contact from store level through online support. That's why so many savvy consumers, including Boomers, pay a premium price for their products.

Make Your Product Part Of Each Boomer's Life Story

Every life, be it a person's or a product's, is made up of a series of tales. Simple storytelling is an ancient art that has resonated with human beings since long before Beowulf. Stories have more meaning and staying power than glib slogans and goofy commercials, because they can touch a deeper place, like the Boomer Buying Center.

So, do a creative exploration, and discover ways to craft stories about how your product intersects with the lives of Boomers. Make them laugh, make them cry, make them feel something about your product, and you'll have created a priceless connection with Boomers that money can't buy.

Ideal Boomer? Trusting intuition? Making creative leaps? If all this is beginning to sound a bit daunting, don't despair. Fortunately, there's a communication tool called the Boomer Strategy Blueprint, and it will help you lay a solid foundation for all of your advertising and marcom.

The Boomer Strategy Blueprint™

The Key To Unlocking Hidden Profits

*T*he Boomer Strategy Blueprint is a proprietary tool that can help you reassess and reposition your products and services in order to transform the way Baby Boomers think, feel and behave in relation to them. The Blueprint gathers the most critical information in key categories and distills it all into a Big Idea that can help your brand carve out a share of mind that will lead to a share of the Boomer market. Here are the categories included in the Blueprint followed by instructions on how to complete them.

Key Facts

These provide a snapshot of prevailing market conditions, including the challenges and opportunities that the brand faces when marketing to Boomers. As a whole, they create a Petri dish in which the brand will either thrive or die.

Who's Your Ideal Boomer?

The better you can define and visualize the perfect prospect for your brand, the more successfully you can focus on connecting in meaningful ways. So, describe your Ideal Boomer in meticulous detail demographically, economically, socially, psychologically and spiritually. Then ask, How do the Ideal Boomer's values shape his or her beliefs about the brand?

What Does Your Brand Stand For?

What makes this particular product or service a unique and exceptional value for Boomers? Why should it be top-of-mind when they consider their needs and wants? Why should it command their loyalty in an increasingly cluttered and cutthroat marketplace?

Competition

Even if the brand seems to own the market, there's always

competition for available dollars. Campbell's owns about 70% of the "wet soup" market, but in addition to other soups, it also competes with countless other convenient foods that Boomers can choose from.

Problem The Big Idea Must Solve

This is the communication challenge as seen through the brand's eyes, not the prospect's. All brands have limitations. State them clearly, directly and honestly, and you'll be able to address the question, Why aren't more Boomers buying what we're selling?

Communication Objective of The Big Idea

This is all about convincing the Ideal Boomer to listen to what you're saying. Carefully consider the brand's overall message as you look through the prospect's eyes. Why should that person pay any attention to what you're saying? Exactly how do you propose to serve that person's needs and interests? What's in it for that person to consider buying whatever you're selling, whether it's a product, a service or an idea? Always remember that if the brand isn't speaking directly to the heart of the Boomer's needs, it's talking to itself.

What Important Benefits Should The Big Idea Promise?

What puts the Boom in your brand? What's the strongest believable claim you can make that will motivate prospects to become customers?

Why Should Boomers Believe The Promise?

What credible statements can the brand make to support its claims?

Other Considerations

When you communicate the Big Idea, is there anything in particular that must be included or excluded? For instance, a look and feel that follows certain graphic standards.

Now that you know what goes into the Blueprint, all you have to do is brainstorm each category, then summarize and synthesize the information into a Big Idea. The result can prove to be very rewarding for your brand, as well as your bottom line.

In the next chapter, we'll take about brainstorming and other creative skills that you'll need to master in order to fill in all those blank spaces.

The Brain Game

How To Brainstorm Your Way To A Big Idea

*E*ach category of the Boomer Strategy Blueprint described in the last chapter will lead to valuable insights into how you can reposition your products and services against the most suitable segment of the Baby Boomer market. That's why you need to put a great deal of effort into gathering and assessing the most important information for each category. Do that, and you'll end up with a Big Idea that can help your brand carve out a bigger share of mind, as well as a bigger share of the Boomer market. And it all starts with brainstorming.

Brainstorming is like panning for gold. You dredge up as

many raw ideas as you can from the depths of your mind and sift them through your emotions and intellect, keeping a keen eye out for the shiniest nuggets.

When you've discovered a bright, new idea, you polish it up and show it off to the world by using it as the Big Idea that makes your product or service really shine. This Big Idea will form the foundation for the basic concept that drives all of your advertising and marcom, from billboards to brochures to TV to Tweets.

Generating ideas on demand takes some practice, but once you get the hang of it, you'll have so many to choose from that you may find it difficult to distinguish a genuinely Big Idea from one that's merely brilliant. But don't worry, there's a virtually foolproof way to distinguish the best from the rest. That's important, because if you're selling to Boomers, you're trying to motivate sophisticated consumers who won't fall for the same old tired pitch. You've got to convince them that your product or service is worthy of their time, attention and dollars. Do that, and you have a chance to turn them into loyal customers for life.

Here's what I call The Big Boom Test for determining if you've got a genuinely Big Idea—one that's powerfully resonant and believable enough to form a solid foundation for all of your communications.

If the Big Idea startles you, or better yet, scares you,
then you've got the real thing, so make the most of it.

Don't be timid and settle for less than the best. Old, "pre-driven" ideas are so comfortable that they just sit there like overstuffed easy chairs and lull Boomers to sleep. That's why they make terrible candidates for building credible, compelling advertising and marketing communication campaigns. If your idea is fresh enough to get everybody around you a little worried, you've made an important discovery. Use it wisely and well.

As you brainstorm, keep in mind that getting Big Ideas can be as quirky and individualistic as the people involved, so the following simple 10-point system is a starting point rather than a set of hard and fast rules. As you develop other ways to discover truly creative ideas, supplement the list with your own personal brainstorming wisdom. Over time, you'll build a skill set that will prove to be indispensable to building your brand and your bottom line.

Ten Steps To Brainstorming Success

Big Ideas are the heart and soul of effective communication, but discovering them is hard work. As the leader of a brainstorming session, you need to know how to sift through the dross in search of those rare nuggets that you can use to create effective advertising and marcom for your products and services. Just remember, you've got to be truly original because Baby Boomers have seen and heard it all. So, roll up your sleeves, loosen up your mind and let's have a brainstorm.

1. **State the problem clearly.** Doing this is sometimes the most challenging—and always the most important—part of the process.

2. **Dig broadly and deeply for solid facts,** because they are the bricks and mortar you will use to create your Big Idea.

3. **Suspend judgment, then free associate.** Quickly capture all of your thoughts on paper (or screen) without assessing their merits.

4. **Collaborate with other bright people.** Strive for a meeting of the minds. And remember that brainstorming should be fun, so use your sense of humor to keep things loose. Laugh out loud at the obvious duds, especially your own.

5. **Focus on the solution.** Begin to objectively judge the raw concepts. Steadily strive for the perfect solution no matter how impossible it may seem.

6. **Innovate in a way that's genuinely original.** But don't get discouraged if you feel you've fallen a bit short of the ideal. As Leo Burnett said, "When you reach for the stars, you may not quite get one, but you won't come up with a handful of mud either."

7. **Choose the best idea.** As group leader, you've got to crown the champ without regard for egos or corporate politics that might muddle the process. In the end, you've got to decide which idea best communicates in a way that's clear, concise, cogent and creative.

8. **Devise a way to sell your Big Idea.** No matter how bril-

liant it may be, a Big Idea doesn't sell itself. That's why you have to showcase it in an exciting, engaging way that makes it come to life. Radiate enthusiasm—it's contagious.

9. **Be flexible, reasonable, honest and courageous.** You're bound to run into objections, so allow for different points of view. In fact, you should encourage and accept constructive criticism, so listen carefully to other opinions. But don't give up on your Big Idea unless there's a truly compelling reason.

10. **Banish the fear of failure.** This is often the single biggest obstacle people must overcome when brainstorming and selling ideas. Keep in mind that being creative isn't for the faint-hearted, so don't worry, just do it. Home run hitters strike out a lot, but that doesn't stop them from swinging for the fences. So make like The Babe, because one Big Idea is worth a thousand "safe" ones that are timeworn and tired. Besides, safe ideas can be downright dangerous to a brand's health. Try slipping one of those safe ideas by a savvy Baby Boomer, and you'll quickly discover what it means to be ignored.

Now that you've got a simple, straightforward guide to brainstorming, start using it today. If you're unsure about how to make the process flow efficiently and effectively, hire an experienced facilitator, preferably someone with training in group dynamics, as well as creative advertising. And to ensure that your Big Idea resonates with Boomers, seek the advice of a qualified gerontology counselor. In addition to contributing unique insights, a professional like that can help keep things moving productively by recognizing and resolving the inevitable roadblocks that spring up whenever people try to build a consensus in a group setting.

In the final analysis, brainstorming is never easy, but when it's done well, it can give birth to a Big Idea that can take your brand to the next level in terms of image and sales, even with a tough group like the Boomers.

Once you have your Big Idea, you need to determine a key question: What's your best position? We'll address that in the next chapter.

What's Your Best Position?

Settling on a Big Idea is just the beginning of the creative process. A Big Idea will only be useful if you can devise a way to transform it into a meaningful platform for all of your advertising and marketing communications. To do that, you need to articulate your Big Idea in a way that leverages its marketing magic, helping your brand create and occupy a unique niche in the mind of the Baby Boomer. So, let's take a closer look at how the power of a Big Idea can be used to carve out a memorable position in the Boomer Buying Center.

WHAT'S THE BIG IDEA?

That's the question Baby Boomers ask themselves whenever they see or hear your advertising or marketing communications. They may not put it in those exact words, but you can be sure that if your message doesn't have the power of a Big Idea behind it, you're fighting a losing battle.

Fortunately, if your brainstorming was successful, then you've got a Big Idea that dramatizes what your brand is all about. And that Big Idea promises to pave the way to the Boomer Buying Center—if you use it in dynamic and effective ways. Your next challenge is to communicate the Big Idea so creatively that it grabs Boomers' attention, and resonates so meaningfully that it motivates them to listen, to act and to buy.

If you think I'm overemphasizing the importance of a Big Idea, consider its power. Skeptics have often asked me, "What's a Big Idea worth?" Although I abhor cigarettes, I cite the example of Marlboro Country. That was a Big Idea that created so much cash flow that it helped build Philip Morris into a multinational behemoth.

How does an idea like a cowboy smoking a cigarette—something that's totally alien to the life of the average person—move so many to buy Marlboros? Who knows?

But it remains a smashing success story, and it still attracts countless consumers despite the fact that the cigarette industry as a whole kills hundreds of thousands of its very best customers every year. Year after year. Amazing. But that's the power of a Big Idea.

Most Big Ideas are a lot more consumer friendly. Take the Maytag Loneliest Man in Town, an advertising icon created by my father Vincent R. Vassolo during his Burnett days. Ol' Lonely really helped put Maytag on the map, and led the brand to the top of its category, where it reigned for decades. It eventually toppled from the pinnacle around the time somebody decided that this marketing communication icon just wasn't effective enough to sell the brand any longer, at least not by using the print stories and TV mini-dramas that emphasized the brand's dependability in such a memorable way.

Go to the Maytag website, and you'll find that they still talk about dependability, and the Loneliest Man is still kicking around somewhere, but he's not front and center, as he was in the days when the brand was dominant. In short, they've neglected their Big Idea to the point where it's lost its creative power.

Years ago, when consumers asked "What's The Big

Idea about Maytag?," they remembered the message of the Loneliest Man In Town, and recalled that the brand stood for rock solid dependability. Now that message is diluted and diffuse, and Maytag seems like just another appliance manufacturer. At this rate, the guy trying to sell the brand at retail may end up being the Loneliest Man In Town.

The lesson is clear. Once you've created your Big Idea, you've got to be very wise in the way you use it and care for it as the years pass. Do right by it, and your Big Idea will help keep your brand top of mind with Boomers, and that's sure to increase sales.

By now I trust you're beginning to appreciate the selling power of a Big Idea. You need one to drive your creative executions; otherwise, clever headlines, countless features and benefits bullets, and cutting-edge production techniques will all add up to advertising and marcom that's flat as a flounder. Don't get me wrong. Superb executional techniques are necessary, but they're certainly not sufficient, because if you don't have a Big Idea behind the magic curtain, you're pushing water uphill.

A Big Idea gives you the leverage needed to penetrate the natural apathy Baby Boomers have toward every brand. Used clearly, concisely and creatively, it can help convince

Boomers to carefully consider whatever you're selling. So why are there so few Big Ideas in advertising and marcom today?

The reason's simple. Big Ideas take guts to implement because they're so fresh and innovative that they're scary. Comfort-seeking marketers shy away from powerful Big Ideas without even realizing that it's the tension that they create that makes them so effective. Big Ideas make people feel and think differently. They smash preconceptions, shatter indifference and dare people to try (or at least consider) something new. In the depths of their souls, Big Ideas are risky business. That's what gives them spirit, and it's that spirit that connects with Boomers.

Going back to the Marlboro example, ask yourself, Is there any sensible reason why a smoker should relate to a cowboy puffing on a cigarette while riding a horse in God-Knows-Where, Montana? I can think of no logical reason. I can barely come up with a semi-convincing subliminal reason. Yet the spirit of that Big Idea has resonated so profoundly over decades that countless smokers around the world have switched to the brand. And who knows how many started smoking because of it?

No one can deny that this particular Big Idea ultimately

proved horribly harmful to millions (the original Marlboro Man purportedly died of lung cancer). However, that fact just puts an exclamation point on the overwhelming power of a truly Big Idea. It's seemingly stonger than life itself!

Is implementing a Big Idea worth the risk? Advertising history suggests it is. Playing table stakes with a Big Idea is never easy, but often the gamble has paid off in a big way and made more than a few daring people look like advertising geniuses. Way back when, it took real courage for Bill Bernbach to tell Avis that it had to overtly admit to being the number two car rental company. Of course, he didn't sheepishly state this obvious fact, and then skulk off into oblivion. Instead, he made that fact—and the Big Idea that grew out of it—the brand's most potent strength.

Bernbach's insistence on using his Big Idea (various versions of, We're number two. We have to try harder) was so bold that he almost lost the Avis account, but he stuck to his creative guns.

The campaign he created was so deliciously different at the time that it became an instant advertising classic. More important, of course, it also helped Avis carve out a unique share of mind that led to a nice, big share of the market. In the end, this oh-so dangerous and heretical idea proved to be a very effective way to drive the company's advertising and marcom, as well as its sales.

My all-time favorite Big Idea was for Sears Diehard Batteries. (I wish I'd been part of the team that came up with it, but I worked on Sears Steady Rider Shocks, instead.) The Big Idea was: "Diehard. Starts Your Car When Most Batteries Won't." Nothing fancy about it. Simple, straightforward and powerfully memorable. It tells you exactly what the product does, and why you can trust it. Every Big Idea should be so good. And how about the name? It's the perfect complement to the Big Idea. "Diehard" says it all.

Of course, after the Diehard breakthrough, Sears gave us the task of coming up with something just as memorable for SteadyRiders. The Big Idea for that brand worked well with the name, but it was no Diehard. (For you advertising historians, it was "SteadyRiders. They named it right." Good, but not great.)

Enough history. Now let's take a close, critical look at your most recent advertising and marcom efforts. Spread them out on the conference room table, and ask, "What's the big idea?" If it hits you right between the eyes, then it will rivet your audience's attention to your sales message. On the other hand, if there's just a lot of noise and flash and mind-numbing detail but nothing really compelling about the sum total of what you're looking at, then it's DOA.

But don't expect your Big Idea to perform miracles all by itself. Like Marlboro, Diehard, et al, you'll need to dramatize that Big Idea with memorable creative executions. There's nothing quite like the magic of creativity to make your Big Idea really come to life in the minds of the Boomers. And when that happens, your brand will be headed straight for the Boomer Buying Center, where all sales begin.

But before you can convince Boomers you're worthy of their time and attention, you need to answer a very important question...

What's Your Best Position?

Creative positioning is crucial to gaining market share, because it helps differentiate products and services in the minds of Baby Boomers. A well-conceived position can penetrate Boomer apathy, and that's an absolute prerequisite for success, because everyone ignores tons of advertising and marketing communications every single day. It's simple self-defense. The relentless promotional bombardment comes from all sides, battering us 24/7, and so much of it sounds and looks the same. But a sharp marketer can rise above the masses and get its message across if it uses its Big Idea as the basis for a position that resonates with Boomers in a uniquely memorable way.

Despite what some marketers seem to believe, positioning isn't something that happens in the marketplace like an end cap display. It happens in each Boomer's mind. Ultimately, that's where all sales occur, so the most innovative positioning is designed to cut through the communication clutter and carve out a unique niche in the Boomer's awareness. But to be effective, it has to be done deftly.

A truly meaningful position doesn't beat people over the head. In fact, some of the most successful positioning is so subtle it's hard to detect. The understated approach is particularly important when selling to Boomers, because they've grown weary of bombastic advertising and marcom that tries to shout over the competition. The secret of effective positioning, then, is to first create a quiet corner in your prospect's mind, and then gently fill it with your message. Speak softly and carry a Big Idea.

Keep in mind that in a world deluged with me-too communications, there's no hope for the marketer with an identity crisis. To carve out a solid position, your brand must know exactly what it's all about, because if you can't figure that out, no one else will either.

Once you've decided on your best position, your next job is to communicate it clearly and creatively in a cogent theme that helps build a distinctive brand personality that resonates with Baby Boomers. Only then will you be able to get the share of mind required to get a healthy share of the Boomer market.

As you create your position, don't fall into the Superlatives Trap. Deal in reality. Understate some of your benefits. "We're number 2, we have to try harder" turned out to be a brilliant position for Avis Rent A Car even though it made it appear that the company was taking a backseat to Hertz. The key to its enduring success was a clear and memorable statement of a crucial consumer benefit. It was the promise of a company that vowed to go the extra mile for the customer. In the same vein, you have to create a position that convinces Boomers that you'll try harder to please them in every possible way, from the quality of your products through customer service and beyond.

And once you've established your position, you have to be consistent. In the mid-seventies, Seven-Up crafted a very intriguing position when it called itself the UnCola. This position succeeded in sharply differentiating the brand, setting it apart from major competitors. Rather than consistently building on this strong position through the years, however, Seven-Up eventually defaulted to the tired soft drink technique of lifestyle advertising, with predictable results.The lesson is clear: If you vacillate, so will your customer base.

More recently, KFC resurrected the Un- idea, asking consumers to UnThink what they know about the kind of chicken the company sells. Although this is clearly derivative, it will make a very interesting case study because the brand seems to be intent on at least partially unseating a well-established idea—KFC = fried chicken—and replacing it with a new line extension concept, KFC = grilled chicken, too. This is tricky business, because they certainly don't want to switch people over to grilled chicken in a way that cannibalizes their flagship product. It will be interesting to see if they can pull it off.

Establishing the best possible position is especially crucial for retailers. During peak promotional periods, most of these businesses look and sound the same because they all articulate very similar shrill messages. (Buy Now! Save Money! Do This Or Die!) And almost all of this shouting is done in an embarrassingly uncreative way. The problem with this myopic approach is that if you look and sound like you're just one of the rabble, you'll never become a leader.

Although it's true that positioning isn't easy, if you can manage to stake out a unique niche in the Boomers' collective consciousness (maintaining a firm foothold in the subconscious, as well), you'll have a share of mind that nothing else can occupy, and that's the key to increasing your share of market.

Bottom line: Effectively answer the question, "What's Your Best Position?" and you'll take an important step toward the Boomer Buying Center.

Creative GeroMarketing™ Basics

*O*nce you've devised a unique position based on your Big Idea, you'll need to execute your advertising and marcom as clearly, concisely, cogently and creatively as possible. Much of what follows in this book will be devoted to providing theories, tactics, techniques and tips that will help ensure that your creative executions will be more effective tools for turning Boomers into buyers.

Four Fundamentals That Will Help You Reach Baby Boomers

Effective advertising and marketing communications depend

on a number of skills that are similar to those that gerontology counselors use. They may hate to admit it, but cut through the dense academic jungle, and you'll find that many of the most popular and effective counseling paradigms follow a process that resembles personal selling.

Of course, there are crucial differences between counseling and selling. Authentic psychosocial counseling is inevitably much more complex and volatile than the sales process, and the outcome is far more significant than dollars gained or lost. Furthermore, attempting to follow the ground rules of professional counseling ethics would quickly and permanently cripple any marketer or advertiser. Despite those crucial differences, it's still useful to consider some of the skills that form the foundation for effective person-to-person communication.

In 1994, there was no name for the marriage of gerontology counseling and marketing communications, so I named it GeroMarketing. Not too catchy, but descriptive nonetheless. No matter what you call it, master these four basic GeroMarketing skills, and you'll be well on your way to reaching the Boomer Buying Center, and that can prove to be a very rewarding journey.

- Establish rapport
- Listen actively
- Use research to form hypotheses about Boomers
- Communicate meaningfully

It would be easy to write volumes about each of the above, but a more important goal is to understand their essence, so you can easily wrap your mind around these concepts and begin to use them effectively in your advertising and marcom. If, in the final analysis, it all seems a bit too touchy-feely for you, find someone who has a solid counseling skill set, as well as the advertising and marcom experience to help you accomplish your goals.

Establish Rapport

Essentially, establishing rapport is all about making friends. And as everyone knows, people like to buy from people they like.

In counseling, establishing rapport is the process of building a continuing relationship based on respect, intellectual and emotional understanding and empathy. Once established, it encourages the client to trust the counselor and become open and receptive to therapeutic approaches. Without rapport, the chance that counseling will succeed is slim, indeed, although you'd never know it from the way some hyperaggressive talk show "counselors" act.

When communicating with Baby Boomers, establishing rapport is the first step on the road to the Boomer Buying Center. It's the key to getting Boomers involved with your advertising and marcom, and it's crucial to all the sales techniques that come after it. But be careful. It can't be done in an obvious, ham-handed way, or it will be perceived as nothing more than crass manipulation. And that means No Sale.

Authentic rapport convincingly mirrors the values and world views of the target market, as well as their communication style and diction level. If you ignore these guidelines and try to willfully impose your message on Boomers, you'll lose them faster than you can say, "Hey, how come that expensive slick brochure didn't work?"

However, if you can make Boomers feel genuinely understood, they will be more apt to trust you and be open to whatever you're selling, because you've shown that you truly comprehend and respect the way that they see the world. Make it clear that you embrace their values—that you're on the same wavelength cognitively and emotionally—and you'll establish the kind of rapport that mere money can't buy. The bottom line is that real rapport has the power to turn Boomers into more than just friends—it can make them loyal customers, too.

Listen With Your Third Ear

Active listening is tricky, because unless you're in a personal selling situation, you're not actually face-to-face with the customer. That means in order to discern what Baby Boomers are "saying," you have to rely on research. But can you really depend on it? Ageism is so pervasive that you need to have the acute sensitivity of a gerontology counselor to tease out the valid from the invalid, the truth from the prejudice. Fortunately, we each have a third ear that allows us to hear in more discerning ways. However, to be useful, the third ear has to be trained to be a finely tuned instrument of active listening.

Active listening can be traced back to Carl Rogers's client-centered therapy. In counseling, its purpose is to listen so attentively that the therapist can reflect back to the speaker what was heard with a high degree of accuracy. It's a skill well worth developing, because it's very useful in countless contexts beyond the therapeutic milieu.

In fact, you can use the principles of active listening to

help you develop and implement your marketing communications with Baby Boomers. Learning to use your third ear will help you see the facts and figures derived from Boomer research in a new light. It will give you a more sensitive understanding of the concepts behind the numbers, as well as the feelings associated with them. When you make a concerted effort to be aware of your preconceived notions, feelings and opinions, you can hear a more accurate kind of truth which goes beyond the numbers and helps you understand and reach Boomers more effectively.

Next time you're assessing research, be it quantitative or qualitative, review these four concepts from gerontology counseling to help fine-tune your third ear. They'll help you form conclusions that resonate with Boomers in ways that facts and figures can't.

Empathy happens when you penetrate external perspectives and break through to a clearer understanding of the Boomer's internal frame of reference. As an empathic listener, you'll understand the Boomer's thoughts and feelings in a way that paints a more accurate picture than the obvious conclusions you might otherwise draw from the research.

Acceptance is empathy's kissin' cousin. It entails having respect for each Boomer simply for being him or herself. And when it's unconditional, it's a powerful relationship builder, because everyone loves to be loved for just being. Acceptance will help you avoid making value judgments about what the Boomer believes. That, in turn, will encourage the Boomer to let his or her defenses down and become more receptive to hearing what you have to say.

Congruence is about being genuine, open and candid. As a congruent listener, you know yourself because you're in touch with your thoughts and feelings. Rather than pretending to be objective, you don't mask emotions, you communicate with genuine candor. In advertising and marcom, being that real is exceedingly rare. But Boomers are good at sniffing out artificiality and insincerity, so keep it real.

Concreteness means focusing on specifics rather than generalities. Be precise about facts, figures, anecdotes—anything you use to try to persuade Boomers to consider what you're selling. That doesn't mean you can't take creative flights of fancy. You just have to make sure that ultimately you return to earth and connect with something real that resonates with Boomers. In the end, being vague is unconvincing. Reality is the only place where productive communication can grow.

Learning to listen actively isn't easy, but it will help

smooth out the often bumpy road to the Boomer Buyer Center. Make the effort, and you'll reap the rewards.

Use Research To Form Hypotheses About Boomers
In gerontology counseling, the counselor's active listening and accurate feedback skills enable clients to clarify issues, so they can effectively address them by using powerful inner resources like insight and problem-solving. Before that can happen, however, the most salient issues have to be identified. Often, this is a problem for both client and counselor. To meet this challenge, counselors form hypotheses about the client's behavior after assessing its overt manifestations and intuitively "researching" its hidden roots.

Marketers must do essentially the same thing before attempting to craft advertising and marketing communications for Baby Boomers. The biggest flaw in forming marketing hypotheses based on research is that too often intuition and creativity are shunned in favor of the "safety of numbers," as if attitudes and values can be accurately measured like height and weight.

Instead of focusing on questions like "What are the most common characteristics of Boomers?" or "What can we do for Boomers?," it's more useful to ask "How does this

Boomer perceive him or herself, and what particular beliefs and values drive his or her motivation?" If you form your marketing hypotheses while looking through the subjective eyes of individual Boomers, you can use your creativity to intuitively connect with what drives their behavior.

The problem is that this seems dangerous if not impossible for most marketers. You can hear their despair in the common lament "I'm just not creative." That's a cop out. Everybody's creative.

What separates creative pros from the rest is the ability to confidently and consistently tap into the imaginative power that all human beings are born with. Learn that skill, trust that power, and you'll be able to boldly form hypotheses about Boomers that will lead you to the Boomer Buying Center.

Communicate Meaningfully

There are as many definitions of what's meaningful as there are people. In gerontology counseling, meaningful communication is crucial because it deepens the therapeutic relationship and helps people understand the roots of conflict, as well as ways to resolve it.

Meaningful communication is equally important when

advertising to Baby Boomers. Perhaps the key thing to keep in mind is that there can be no pat formula for meaningful communication, because each encounter that a marketer has with a Boomer is a unique experience for both. Often, you have to play it by ear—your third ear, that is. The one that's so sensitive that it lets you "hear" what the other two so often miss.

Of course, there are countless ways to meaningfully communicate with Boomers, but for openers, I'll offer just a handful of thought starters. In no particular order then, here are twenty tidbits to consider.

1. If you don't talk directly to the Boomers' individualism, you're talking to yourself.

2. Substance trumps style.

3. Authenticity puts trendiness to shame.

4. Self-awareness increases your ability to speak with conviction.

5. Humility is important because communication can be a mysteriously complex and uncertain process.

6. Your personal assumptions and interpretations have to take a backseat to what Boomers actually feel, believe and value.

7. Create a positive connection.

8. Find a deft way to combine emotional and intellectual appeals.

9. Don't be afraid to challenge Boomers. They admire self-confidence.

10. Be creative. Offer fresh perspectives, innovative angles, new insights and provocative opinions.

11. Offer a Big Idea that Boomers can wrap their minds around and act on.

12. Be cogent. Make your message so compelling that Boomers will motivate themselves to listen to what you're saying.

13. Be concise. Nobody likes a windbag, so don't use two words when one will do.

14. Be clear. Revise your writing over and over and over again until your message is perfectly lucid.

15. Create a change, whether it's in belief, attitude or emotion. Inform, inspire, enrage, educate, just don't be namby pamby.

16. Since 1926, McCann Erickson's motto has been "Truth Well Told." Nothing resonates as convincingly as reality.

17. Strive to communicate in a way that makes Boomers think, "You took the words right out of my mouth."

18. Don't insult the Boomers' intelligence by talking down

to them.

19. Avoid stereotypes, especially about age, at all costs.

20. Be true to yourself and what you have to offer.

I could go on, but it would be more productive if you made your own list to supplement the above. As you do, keep in mind that effective communication doesn't happen by accident. Carefully assess every single thing you say and the way you say it in your advertising and marcom, and you should be able to communicate meaningfully with Boomers. And that will open the door to the Boomer Buying Center.

Storytelling Magic

To Gain A Bigger Share Of Mind,

Create A Compelling Story

*A*ll brands are created and live in the human mind, not the bosom of your company. Likewise, all sales begin inside the consumer's head. If you're a marketer, it's important to wholeheartedly embrace this reality, especially if you're selling to Baby Boomers. They're highly individualistic, thoughtful consumers, so they'll form their own attitudes and opinions about your brand and act accordingly. That means you have to be insightful, sensitive and genuine in the way you communicate with them. One of the best ways to reach

Boomers is through a well-wrought brand story.

A good story will grow roots that make people feel increasingly attached to your brand. Its tentacles will reach far beyond any single piece of advertising or marcom. Ultimately, it will envelop each Boomer in a world of meaning where he or she can vividly experience your brand.

Although a story may be more challenging to create than a run-of-the-mill ad or commercial, when you're tying to motivate Boomers, you can't just ride the wave of the latest fad and expect fluff to carry the day. Boomers are far more sophisticated shoppers than Gen Xers and Yers. With Boomers, you actually have to create a brand experience that's worthy of their time, attention and dollars. To gain mindshare with Boomers, you must thoughtfully craft your advertising and marcom in a way that patiently builds your brand's image while attempting to make the sale. One of the most effective ways to do that is through storytelling.

Carving out a share of mind is easy to understand but difficult to accomplish, because it takes considerable talent and time to accomplish the task. Perhaps that's why so many contemporary marketers don't bother, going for the quick hit instead. That may work temporarily for an "On Sale Today Only!" pitch; however, stressing this approach is likely to relegate the brand to the LaBrea Tar Pits of clueless advertisers, where it will wallow with countless other has-beens. Oddly enough, many former powerhouse brands subscribed to share-of-mind advertising and marcom during their glory years. But for some reason, they stopped brand building and lost focus. Eventually, people could no longer relate to their products, resulting in declining share of market and sales.

Companies that are relentlessly focused on hyping rather than brand building, may generate floor traffic by offering inducements garnished with a sense of urgency, but ultimately that myopic approach can be as harmful to a brand's well-being as shoddy products and services.

Almost any business can make a few bucks by shouting "Buy Now Or Die!," but lasting riches come to marketers who make a real effort to create a credible story that captures a brand's personality so vividly that people can come to know and trust it over time. This approach is particularly important when targeting Boomers, because they've reached a developmental stage where they've become more contemplative, valuing long-term relationships over brief flings.

Share-of-mind advertising is more like a courtship than a

sales pitch. It sells gently but persistently, presenting products and services in a way that allows Boomers to decide what the brand actually means and whether it deserves a place in their lives. As confidence in the brand grows, so do profitable sales and brand equity.

When done with flair, imagination, humor and warmth, share-of-mind advertising can transform a parity product into an industry leader. Apple and Nike are just two of the consistent brand builders that dominate sales in their crowded, competitive categories. They've created, nurtured and grown brand stories that are known, respected and loved all around the world, urging people to "Think Different" and "Just Do It!" But those slogans would have been empty vessels without the compelling brand stories that gave them real meaning.

The one thing storytelling brands have in common is a history of doing effective share-of-mind advertising. Through the years they have looked, acted and communicated like credible, reliable leaders, so consumers know them, trust them and buy from them.

So, now that you've discovered your brand's Big Idea and used it to create a unique position that has the power to carve out a niche in the Boomers' awareness, you can begin to build a brand story that will find a place in their hearts and minds, and just as important, in the Boomer Buying Center.

Get Personal

Before building a meaningful brand story, let's take a rough ride with an old-fashioned, high-pressure salesman and see what happens. Picture this: He comes into your home, sits down next to you, and begins talking about his product or service. But he's not particularly warm or friendly. In fact, he subjects you to a rather impersonal sales pitch. It quickly becomes apparent that he has no desire to communicate person to person.

He bores you with an endless list of features that mean little to you. He shouts the price in your face, while braying about what a great deal he's giving you. Then he asks for the order, stressing that it's now or never, because he won't be able to give you such a fabulous bargain tomorrow.

By now, you're not in the mood to do anything but throw him out on his ear. And that's exactly what the vast majority of people do to almost all the advertising and marketing communications that they experience.

People can't be bored or bullied into parting with their money, but sometimes they can be nudged or romanced into buying—if you touch them in a genuinely personal way. This is especially important if you're selling to Baby Boomers. They're highly individualistic, so they like to be tickled where they really live. Of course, determining how to do that takes much more than research. It takes someone with the insight and sensitivity of a counselor and the street smarts of an advertising and marcom pro.

It takes someone like that, because you can't create a feeling of personal warmth with reach and frequency alone. That frame of mind is born of a genuine rapport that you create. And that rapport doesn't come easily. Building it takes time and finesse and a caring attitude that respects each Boomer's needs, desires and self-perceptions.

Our obnoxious salesman isn't the type who would bother trying to develop such a "soft" skill set. Why bother, when you can bulldoze people? Well, that might have worked with some consumers in the past, but not Boomers. That's why your advertising and marcom need to go far beyond canned presentations—the kind that bore the audience with drivel that was cobbled together by a committee back at the home office. Before you take this route, ask yourself, When has anything genuinely personal come out of a committee?

Whatever media you use, the message is clear: People

are always more open to what you're saying and selling when you converse with them, not talk at them. Faceless facts, no matter how convincing they may seem, don't make for persuasive communication. People rarely buy for purely logical reasons. Most often they use logic to rationalize the emotionally-driven purchasing decision they've already made.

If you decide to get personal with Boomers, just keep in mind that there are ways to shout without yelling. As you create your brand story, ask yourself if it really hits Boomers where they live. Does it express—even embrace—the possibility of Positive Aging? Does it sell gently, with warmth and respect? Does it treat Boomers the way you'd like to be treated by someone coming into your own home? After all, the mind is the most important home we all have.

No matter how you do it, one thing is undeniable: Get personal as you build a brand story with warmth, wit and humanity, and you'll be far more welcome in the Boomer Buying Center.

Once Upon A Time...

The arc of every lifetime is one big story made up of many little ones. That's why the first form of creative communication was storytelling. Storytelling is so important that there's evidence of it in virtually every known culture and subculture throughout human existence. It was, in fact, the most important way to transmit knowledge and wisdom in the millennia before the invention of writing.

Since ancient times, storytelling has been considered an almost magical form of entertainment and education, holding peoples' attention long enough to teach many of life's most important lessons. Its simple, straightforward techniques put to shame most of the "sophisticated" tricks of the trade currently being used in what passes for contemporary advertising and marcom.

We're all familiar and comfortable with storytelling, so it's puzzling why more marketers aren't using its techniques to promote their brands. After all, every product and service has an important and compelling story to tell, and that story is, in fact, what every successful brand is all about.

If you'd like to try promotional storytelling, keep in mind that you must be vividly creative and crystal clear, as well as concise. You also need to be persuasive at a gut level that genuinely resonates with people. Storytelling can be particularly effective with Baby Boomers, because they've reached a developmental stage where they process information more slowly, thoughtfully and carefully than those who constantly twitter about. Their growing penchant for contemplation makes them more open to a persuasive story that has real depth. In fact, with Boomers, nothing works quite as well as storytelling when it comes to holding their attention, educating them about products and services, and motivating them to buy.

Boomers love a good story, which is reason enough for you to search for and crystallize the Big Idea in your product or service into a position that can serve as a solid foundation for your brand story. Done deftly, that story will allow you to dramatize your brand's features and benefits in a compelling and meaningful tale that wends its way into the Boomer Buying Center.

Testimonials are the most obvious form of promotional storytelling, but there's so much more you can do. You can begin by considering your brand to be a character that's intrinsic to the human drama. Think of it as a living, breathing entity that has a life of its own and a backstory that's fascinating and engaging. Explain how the brand got to be what it is today, how it makes the present moment more fulfilling, and how it promises to help build a better tomorrow.

Your brand has a interesting, important story to tell, so

share it with Boomers by showing them how its life intersects with their own. Use a little storytelling magic to create a physical, emotional, social and spiritual bond between your brand and the Boomers, and you'll be well on your way to the Boomer Buying Center.

Telling Your Brand Story

If you want to learn how to be a great commercial storyteller listen to the best. One of the most popular was Paul Harvey. His book, *"The Rest Of The Story,"* is worth its weight in gold for every aspiring storyteller. For decades, Harvey sniffed around the most common places and came up with some of the most uncommonly interesting stories you can imagine. No wonder millions of loyal listeners made him one of the biggest radio personalities in America.

A couple of the stories in the book include the tale of the 20th century presidential candidate who killed a teenage girl, and a New York governor who dressed like a woman—at the electorate's expense, of course. Each line of each story is packed with so much interest, that you can't stop reading. And, of course, there's Harvey's patented surprise punch line that never fails to make you say, "Hey, I didn't know that." The stuff is sheer delight, not to mention a great way to learn memorable information. Wouldn't you love to be able to do something like that for your products and services? Well, you can.

Of course, trying to match Harvey's ingenuity and creativity is pretty daunting, so you might start with something easier, like pourquoi. Pourquoi is French for "why?," and, as the name suggests, these "origin" stories explain how or why something got the way it is. For example, why does a zebra have stripes? It's hard to say, but one thing for sure is that you can create a pretty interesting story explaining it in a plausible and memorable way. The reason these "how and why" stories are so popular is that in addition to being entertaining and informative, they also often reveal the genesis of deep-rooted cultural traditions. That makes them feel like they're part of the audience's DNA, and that makes them comfortably compelling.

So, if you want to put storytelling to work for you, discover the "how and why" of your brand. Then dramatize it in a way that makes it really matter to Baby Boomers. You'll find that if you can tell the right brand story in the right way, you'll be on your way to the pot o' gold at the end of the rainbow: The Boomer Buying Center.

Elements Of A Compelling Brand Story

We've already covered some of the reasons why you should put storytelling to work for your brand when selling to Baby Boomers. Now it's time for some nuts and bolts. The techniques of good storytelling are easy to describe but difficult to master. Still, it pays to consider some of the common characteristics that all good stories share. So, here are some things you should consider as you begin to think about how you might create and tell the story of your brand.

Center On One Clear Theme

Build on a theme that resonates with Baby Boomers, and you'll be able to communicate in a way that seems timeless to them. You can't go wrong by focusing on the possibilities of Positive Aging, while stressing the Boomers' most important values, especially individualism. Think in terms of a big, dramatic idea that you can use in a compelling message that rings true with Boomers on a gut level. And whether you express the theme explicitly or implicitly, make sure that it comes through in a way that showcases its effect on the individual, as well as contemporary life. The theme should also showcase your product as a hero of sorts.

Develop A Dramatic Plot

This may be the most important element, because a brand story needs to have dramatic impact to cut through the communication clutter in today's world. The only way Boomers will pay attention to your story is if you bring out the inherent drama of your brand in a clearly developed sequence of events. To motivate them to embrace your theme, the flow of action must make plot development reasonable and easy to follow.

Craft A Logical Storyline

If you want Boomers to follow your brand story, the plot has to flow in a simple, concise way. You begin by setting the stage for the action to come, then you introduce characters as they become players in the drama of your brand's life story. In the end, the drama builds to a compelling climax, as the brand is positioned as the "hero" that brings the story to a satisfactory resolution. As you tell the story, vary the ebb and flow of the action. Make sure that transitions are smooth, and that characters have every opportunity to interact meaningfully.

Create Realistic Characters

Stories are about characters, so make them seem real, even

if they take on a nonhuman form, like the tortoise and the hare. Storytelling is pointless unless the audience can feel what the characters are experiencing and why. You make characters believable by physically describing them, as well as their actions, thoughts and speech. Well-developed characters encourage the audience to get inside their skin— to empathize and sympathize with them. That's why you must fill your story with lively personalities that others want to know. Breathe life into your characters, and they'll be convincing.

Write With Ear And Eye Appeal

Diction level, sentence structure, voice and content are all important elements of storytelling. Combine them in a way that's appropriate to the audience, and your story will rest easy on the ears, making it all the more welcome to the listener. Imagery and words should always be used in a way that paints a vivid picture of each scenario, helping you establish a mood that harmonizes with the message.

Be Sincere

If you believe in your story and are convinced by it, your audience will be, too. So express yourself in a genuine way that's honest, straightforward and earnest.

Radiate Enthusiasm

Don't confuse this with rah-rah cheerleading and over-the-top excitement. Real enthusiasm springs with genuine gusto from the soul of the story, making your brand lively, interesting and inspiring. If you communicate a passion for your brand, others will feel it, and react accordingly.

Say It With Style

There's nothing wrong with understatement, but if you don't pull it off artfully, you risk boring Boomers, and that's the end of the story. Most of the time, a little pizzazz goes a long way, so speak in a vigorous voice. Make your story spirited, exciting, eye-catching, enchanting. Help Boomers experience everything with their mind's eye, including sounds, tastes, smells and colors, then paint vivid word pictures with vibrant language. Make the audience feel what you're talking about. Make every word the perfect word. Imbue each sentence with a mellifluous rhythm and resonance. And, of course, don't just talk about what's happening, show it.

Respect The Audience

When it comes to advertising and marcom, Boomers have seen and heard it all, so they can be an impatient bunch. Respect their time and attentiveness by telling your brand story as concisely and cogently as possible. And don't clutter your story with too much unnecessary detail. Boomers are bright, well-educated, worldly people, so you can trust them to draw the proper conclusions based on what you've presented. If you think you need to say a lot to be convincing, watch Pixar's *UP*. It provides an ideal example of wordless storytelling in a brief montage of the main character's life from childhood, through marriage and into old age. Without saying a word, it's as meaningful and moving as anything you've ever read or heard. That's why the most gifted storytellers are as well-versed in creating enchanting images as they are in using engaging language.

Keep It Real

This isn't to say that your story can't make a crazy leap or take a flight of fancy (again, see Pixar's *UP*), but the theme and basic message that the audience takes away has to be something they can realistically relate to. The believability factor is crucial to the success of your brand story. So, develop a style that's uniquely yours. Live with your brand story until the characters and their world become as real to you as people and places you've known all your life. Make the story real for yourself, and you'll be able to keep it real for Boomers.

Now that you know what it takes to be a good storyteller, it's time to write the story of your brand. If you feel that you don't have the time or talent, find someone who does, because working a little storytelling magic is one of the most effective ways to connect with Baby Boomers, and that's like money in the bank.

What's In It For Me?

*W*hether spoken or unspoken, that's what every Baby Boomer asks when he or she hears your sales pitch. Boomers are self-centered individualists, so no matter what the medium, from TV to Twitter, their first question is quite naturally "What's in it for me?" If your advertising and marcom aren't answering that query clearly and credibly, you have no right to expect stellar sales. In fact, if you can't tell Boomers what's in it for them, you're talking to yourself, so save your money.

Boomers don't care about your products or services the way you do, so simply talking about their wonderful features is a real snooze. It's like showing complete strangers pictures of your kids and expecting them to respond with more than a polite nod.

The only time you should mention product features is when you can directly and credibly tie them to benefits that promise to change Boomers' lives for the better. Do that and you have a chance to grab and hold their attention, especially if those benefits are related to Positive Aging.

Rather obvious, you say? Then why isn't it common in today's advertising and marcom? I think it's because too many marketers are clueless or complacent. Most seem content to say: "We're great, and you should love us the way we love ourselves." That may work with youthful consumers, but it won't fly with discriminating Boomers.

You can't expect them to be captivated by plain vanilla features and then discern the corresponding benefits automatically. They just aren't going to work that hard to relate to your pitch. If your product or service has a feature important enough to state, then you must clearly attach a meaningful benefit to it, otherwise don't bother mentioning it.

When benefits are vividly highlighted in clear, concise, creative and cogent ways, the full value of what you're offering suddenly seems obvious. Dramatize those benefits, and you may convince Boomers that whatever you're selling will make their lives better in ways they may never have dreamed possible, and that can open the door to the Boomer Buying Center.

Promises, Promises

When Baby Boomers ask, "What's in it for me?," they're looking for a strong Promise and equally strong Reasons Why they should believe it. But your Promise and Reasons Why have to be much more than mere marketing statements. They have to sparkle with creativity, too.

A genuinely creative approach will elevate the Promise and Reasons Why above the commonplace and give them the edge needed to cut through the clutter of today's communications garbage can. Of course, there's no safe, scientific way to be creative, which is why so many marketers shy away from trying. Fact is, you've got to be a risk taker to even dabble in creativity, because seeking safety is antithetical to the creative process.

One reason why being creative is inherently dicey is that it's often hard to differentiate good creative from bad. A quick glance at most current advertising and marcom demonstrates that.

Here's a helpful way to separate potentially breakthrough creative concepts from all the rest: If an idea is both strategically sound and startling, it's probably innovative enough to penetrate the Boomers' apathy. On the other hand, if the idea feels a little too comfortable, pitch it, because it's undoubtedly shopworn. And never worry about being "too creative"—that's impossible. Just make sure that you stay on target, because as the advertising adage goes, "It ain't creative if it don't sell."

If you're interested in tapping into your own creativity to increase the effectiveness of your advertising and marcom, you should understand that it isn't a theoretical or businesslike venture. It's more like jumping into the sandbox and playing. Just make sure that the results include a meaningful Promise that's supported by credible, compelling Reasons Why Boomers should believe it.

If you're not interested in the DIY approach, push those whom you hire to go far beyond the expected. Insist that your ad agency makes use of powerful imagery that persuades the audience to see your products and services in a new light. Tell your creative team that you want to be as competitive as possible without appearing too pushy. Encourage your graphics people to design creative executions that are relevant, uncluttered and stylish. Urge your copywriters to use memorable language to concisely bring out the best in your products with elegant simplicity.

Lead by example. Be daring and a bit presumptuous. Be gutsy and a little dangerous, too. In short, be creative, whatever that means in the context of your communication challenge and business environment. Just make sure that everything you do is believable in a way that resonates on the deepest levels with Baby Boomers.

No matter how you approach the creation of your advertising and marcom, always keep in mind that it must begin and end with a believable Promise. Clearly and credibly communicate that Promise with a boldly executed Big Idea, and eventually you'll break through to the Boomer Buying Center. That's a promise.

Hit 'Em In The Gut

When It Comes To Boomer Buying Decisions,

Emotion Trumps Logic

*A*dvertising and marcom are more memorable when they evoke visceral emotions, especially when you're targeting Baby Boomers. It's not that Boomers aren't well educated or intellectually sophisticated enough to make well-reasoned, logical judgments. It's that all of us have a tendency to use logic in order to justify decisions that are rooted in emotion rather than pure rationality. So, if you aim to communicate effectively with Boomers, you've got to hit them where they really live. Pow! Right in the gut.

Conventional wisdom says that we're logical, level-headed people who make enlightened choices based on our ability to analyze information. But it's closer to the truth to say that emotion is reflected in every facet of decision making. Still, we persist in embracing comfortable illusions. So whether it's a sixty-two year old grandma who's a seasoned shopper or a hard-nosed executive, that person probably believes that when he or she buys something, they've done their due diligence and made a businesslike decision after reflecting on all the facts in the cool, calm light of reason. Not likely.

Just remember that when you're trying to sell anyone anything, you've got to give them good reasons to buy, or they won't. And the fact is that more often than not "good reasons" tend to be highly subjective and emotional rather than objective and factual.

Boomers are self-centered individualists with outsized egos, so the most effective communications appeal to what those subjective egos need or want to believe about themselves, others and the state of their world. Objective facts are most important when they support the Boomers' emotional needs, desires and choices.

Even though Boomers grow more contemplative with age, they're highly selective about the facts they use to rationalize and support buying decisions that they've already made at the gut level. Even purchases that seem based on a straightforward thing like saving money are more often linked to what saving money means to the buyer's ego than to the actual value of the dollars saved.

That doesn't mean that emotion has to ooze from every pore of everything you communicate. In fact, your greatest challenge is to portray the emotional appeal in such a subtle way that it works its magic quietly.

And keep in mind that ideas and words aren't the only tools you can use to elicit an emotional response. Any technique that helps you tap into the Boomers' emotions will help you touch the spiritual child that lives within each of them. That's the part of their being that's more playful, less reasonable, less uptight, more spontaneous. You can help create that emotional appeal with colors, shapes and designs that engage and challenge the imagination. You can use rich imagery that conjures up complex feelings that even the most agile mind can't quite grasp intellectually but can certainly discern at a gut level.

Get Creative To Hit Boomers Where They Really Live
One of the biggest problems in assessing advertising and

marketing communications is that creative executions can't be reliably judged by using logic and reason alone. Advertising that makes perfectly good sense to the rational part of the mind is often dull and predictable on a gut level. "But is it effective?," I hear the MBAs screaming. To which I counter, "Did you ever try to bore someone into buying something?" It doesn't work.

If you want to employ creativity in your communications, you have to learn to loosen up. Don't be afraid to entertain "peculiar" ideas, especially ones that seem scary. Use bright, inventive language to give fresh expression to old, familiar things. Be enthusiastic, but don't try to force emotion, because then it will have a whiff of desperation about it. People can smell a phony a mile away, so if you can't swing free and easy and connect on a gut level, hire someone who can, because nothing is more pathetic than a caricature of an emotion.

Of course, I'm not advocating creativity for its own sake. Unfettered creativity can be quite destructive at times. The current global financial catastrophe is firmly rooted in the creativity of mortgage underwriters and the seductive but worthless securities that a cadre of quantitative geniuses created out of thin air. To be useful, creativity has to be disciplined by good judgment and uncommon sense, the kind born of innate talent.

If you want to hit Baby Boomers in the gut with your message, your creative executions must be built on a solid strategic foundation. Then you have to creatively massage that strategy until it yields the emotional appeal that you can use to motivate browsers to become buyers.

Once you've got a grip on the gut-level appeal you want to use, you have to put the primary emotional benefit right up front—in your ad's headline, in the first three seconds of your radio and TV commercials, on the cover of your direct mail. In short, you've got to take a straightforward approach to hit 'em right in the gut.

Sudden emotional impact has real stopping power that engages the audience and motivates them to take action. This leads to more than just increased sales and bigger profits, it also helps build customer loyalty, because Boomers will feel that you understand them on a level that few others do.

Ultimately, to get to that special place called the Boomer Buying Center, where all purchasing decisions are made, you have to be half intuitive counselor and half creative communications genius. If you've got both of those things going for you, you'll understand how to discover and stay on the right wavelength in a way that will resonate with Boomers, making them far more receptive to your messaging.

Begin By Taking Your Own Emotional Pulse

Of course, developing the skills of a sensitive, creative communicator doesn't happen overnight. Not only do you have to have an inborn creative spark, you also have to learn to tap into the source of your creativity, and that's not easy. A good way to start is to pretend you're a counselor in training.

Begin by getting in touch with yourself. Jump into the deep end of your emotional swimming pool. Learn to recognize what a genuine emotion feels and looks like, how you react to it, and how your reactions affect others.

Once you've learned to take your emotional pulse, keep your finger on it. Practice expressing your feelings with a colorful and diverse vocabulary. Talk about your emotions. Write about them. Draw what you feel. Be genuinely expressive! Do this consistently, and you'll begin to realize your creative potential. Make a real effort, and your natural creative spark will explode into brilliance, illuminating every aspect of your life with a richness born of limitless creative possibilities.

If it sounds like a lot of work, well, it is. That's why

most people won't bother. That puts you in the driver's seat, however, because even if you end up with results that aren't quite magical, you'll still be miles ahead of the rest.

Too many people try to substitute academic degrees and book learning for true creative exploration. That's why so much of today's advertising and marcom is pablum. The truth is that creativity comes from the depths of the spirit not the pages of a book or a classroom lecture. And if you think there's safety in doing things the way everybody else does, you're wrong, because seemingly safe creative executions are actually dangerous to your bottom line, particularly when you're going after Boomers.

If you want to increase profitable sales, you'll have to learn to be more creative, not more rational. You may be able to think your way to sound marketing strategies, but you can't "think" people into buying, especially Boomers. Emotions have far more impact and persuasive power than mere logic and reason. So, to create more effective communications, start with a sound strategy, vest it with genuine emotion, and hit 'em in the gut.

Boomers Love Brands
With Personality

What's Your Brand's PQ?

*D*oes your brand have a high Personality Quotient (PQ)? That's a key question, because when you're selling to Baby Boomers, they consistently seek out products and services that are believable and likeable, just like the people they trust most. That's why one of your primary marketing goals should be to build a credible, friendly image using a variety of creative marketing communications, from advertising to PR to tweeting.

A brand's image is the personality that it projects. Like the Boomers, the best brand personalities are highly individualistic, while the worst try to be all things to all

143

people and end up being buried beneath the clutter of the teeming marketplace. To avoid this fate, you must raise your brand's PQ by reaching out and touching Boomers where they really live. Do that, and over time, they'll embrace your brand, as well as your entire company, as you gain an ever larger share of mind and market.

Many of the most effective image builders come from direct marketing. Take a pioneer like L.L. Bean and a more recent success story like Victoria's Secret, for example. These brands appeal to decidedly different market segments, and in their own ways, they've built highly individualistic brand personalities that their customers have come to know and trust. Their high PQs have helped them carve out a share of mind by standing for something uniquely important to their customers. That's why they continue to be successful, maintaining their fiscal fitness even when the broader economy falters.

PQ Doesn't Stand For Pretty Quick

Effective brand building takes time. It's a process that is measured in years and decades, not weeks and months. It's characterized by patient relationship building aimed at people who might become loyal customers. It avoids profit-shredding special promotions that appeal to bargain hunters who are constantly sniffing out the best deal du jour.

Although it's true that icons like Coke might be able to survive cost-cutting branding initiatives in certain times and places, those tactics only work with megabrands which have an established image that only a catastrophe could damage.

Of course, there are some challenges that no brand PQ can survive unscathed. A good example is Toyota's recent tsunami of quality and PR disasters that have rapidly transformed the brand from a Jekyll into a Hyde. And BP has also taken a breakneck slide down a slippery slope of its own making. Whether its initials change to BK remains to be seen, but if it survives as a brand, it will be rehabilitating its image for years if not decades to come.

Unlike some brands which seem to change with the seasons, L.L. and Victoria keep burnishing the same image, year after year. These brands raise their PQs slowly but surely, while other advertisers try to rebuild images instantly, as if the sheer weight of megabuck budgets can buy enduring relationships. As a result, they've earned something money can't buy: Customer loyalty.

When you consider how the most successful advertisers build brand images, some important things come to light.

First, many of them personalize their companies by using spokespeople who look and sound credible. Makes sense. After all, it's a lot more comfortable to buy from a human being than a faceless corporation.

They also try to build relationships using potentially high-touch media like direct mail rather than mass media like TV, because the more intimate the contact, the more it will resonate with the target market. Genuine warmth goes a long way in selling Baby Boomers on specific brands, which is why they value companies with high PQs.

Marketers with high PQs resonate with Boomers because they treat them like reasonable people. They value their feelings as much as their intellects. Like everyone else, Boomers like to be treated with simple respect, and when a business offers that, they reciprocate with increased loyalty as they come to know and trust the company and its brands.

Like dependable people, companies with the highest PQs aren't fickle, so they don't change images every year or two. Instead, they build on their existing one. This gives them genuine credibility, so when they claim a long history of satisfying customers, Boomers know that they can back up those claims with believable evidence like testimonials. This helps the brand's image grow broadly and deeply, laying

146

down roots in the Boomer Buying Center over time.

All this brand building helps companies leverage their ad dollars, too, because with each passing year, they're strengthening facets of their existing PQ rather than spending incremental dollars on an expensive facelift or complete makeover.

Like people with strong personalities, companies with the highest PQs know who they are and what they're about, so they stand behind their products and services with iron-clad, no-risk, money-back policies. They make a commitment to customer satisfaction and back it with a "no-questions asked" guarantee, because they know that's how you build trust.

Companies with high PQs also manage to do a better job of image building because they refuse to waste time or money on marketing communications that don't work. Rather than drowning the market with saturation messaging, they try to consistently reach out to their best prospects with pinpoint communications that go right to the heart of each Boomer's self-interest.

So, to increase your Personality Quotient, build a friendly, believable image—one that will carve out a unique niche in Boomers' minds. Once you've established that position, speak to their individualism with messages than stress the possibilities and benefits of Positive Aging and living in the Now. Do all that and more, and your brand will have the kind of high PQ that Boomers love, and that's a surefire way to get a solid ROI.

Think Like A Copywriter

Why Bother?

*E*ven if you've never aspired to be a copywriter, it pays to think like one when you're courting Baby Boomers. To help with that, I'm going to assume that you'd like to be a DIY copywriter. Now, that may sound far-fetched, but in my experience, it seems like almost anyone who can hold a pencil or tap on a keyboard fancies him or herself a writer. Whether you're like that or not, thinking like a copywriter will help you get the best results from those you employ to create your brand image, advertising, PR and marcom.

Of course, there's a huge difference between dabbling

in writing and living by the written word. I've been a professional writer since the age of 21, and I've learned a few things along the way that I'd like to share with those who aspire to the writer's life, even if that fantasy only lasts for as long as it takes to read this chapter.

First, you should know that the secret to good writing is dogged persistence. Good writing does not mysteriously well up from some cavern of creativity deep within the soul. Nor does it only happen when the muse strikes. In fact, waiting for inspiration paves the way for starvation. Simply put, good writing comes from facts and the ideas that spring from them. Facts provide the who, what, where, when, why and how that fuel the imagination. Once the creative candle is lit, old images and familiar feelings are seen in a new light. When that happens, all things are possible, because they're just a flight of fancy away.

That's true even if you're a commercial writer, as I am. Right now, I'm writing about Baby Boomers, so my ideas and vocabulary tend to focus on individualism and Positive Aging. To sell Boomers with the written word, you must envelop them in facts about your product or service, but you can't bore them into buying. The facts that you present and the way you present them must be captivating, involving, interesting, engaging and important. They have to turn the Boomers' imaginations loose in a way that eventually helps them convince themselves that they need whatever you're selling.

The hallmark of all good writing is the use of concrete language. The kind of language that gets Boomers really close to your product or service. It's the kind of language that let's the Boomer touch it, taste it, experience it on every possible level, physically, emotionally and spiritually. It lets the Boomer dream about your product or service, fantasize about it, fall in love with it.

Finding the most important facts about your product or service isn't always as simple as it may seem. You have to dig, not just deeply but widely. You have to flood every level of your mind with all the facts you can discover. Then suddenly "Pop!", something creative will happen. You'll discover a new relationship that no one else ever saw. Or you'll transform a banal feature into an important and exciting new benefit. With the right touch, a good writer can light up the sky with a meteor shower of new ideas derived from the same old dry facts that everybody else takes for granted.

What you do with your newfound insights will demonstrate if you're a really good creative writer or not. To see how you measure up, fill a blank page with all the facts that you can dig up about your product or service. Build a big list without stopping to critique along the way, then sleep on it. If you're a real writer, you'll hit the ground running the next morning with lots of new permutations and combinations of the stuff you wrote the day before. New ideas and themes will flow through your fingertips and onto the page. If you find you get stuck along the way, don't give up. Real pros know that Writer's Block is more an excuse than a reality. Keep writing, and you'll overcome every obstacle. At least that's been my experience over the past forty-plus years.

Direct response copywriters are the door-to-door salespeople of the writing world. I say that without a trace of sarcasm and with great admiration. These copywriters labor in the vineyard of direct marketing, so they don't depend on dazzling style to make the sale. Instead, they focus on writing the most cogent Because copy possible, because that's what's required to motivate Baby Boomers to take action. Because copy supplies the Reasons Why anyone should give serious consideration to what you're saying and selling. Its purest form might be a short bullet that makes a rather common product feature seem like something that will enhance the

Boomer's life.

Effective Because copy is especially important when talking to direct marketing prospects because they always want to know Why? Why is that such a good feature? Why should I believe the claims that are made? Why is the product worth the price? Why should I buy the product? Direct response copywriters answer each Why with at least one credible, compelling Because, because that's what it takes to convert browsing Boomers into loyal customers.

Direct response writing is the closest thing to "writing as science" that I can think of because its results can be measured to some extent. However, despite what the latest high-priced seminar may claim, there aren't any reliable formulas for successful direct response copywriting, although there are certain guidelines that are usually worth heeding. For instance, research suggests that using certain tricks of the trade can influence response rates in a positive way. There are plenty of good books around that can teach you the basics, but there are no shortcuts to mastering direct response copywriting. It may be part science, but it's part magic, too. And, as with every skill, you learn by doing, refining, doing, refining… It's not easy, but it can be very rewarding.

It's a shame that so many people consider direct response

copywriting to be shilling rather than a serious tool of commerce. This is partly due to simple ignorance, but it's also because some people think that all writing should rise to the level of fine art, whatever that is. Besides being a snooty point of view, it's also misguided. Writing of any kind, from a short poem to a ponderous tome, has always been about selling something, be it an inspiring idea *(Walden),* a defense of a political position (universal healthcare), or costly commercials (*The Super Bowl, 30 Rock*, et al).

A couple of decades ago, an advertising client asked me if I'd ever written anything "serious." I guess she meant a novel, or even less profitable, a short story. Although I've written both, I replied that copywriting is the most serious kind of writing that I do. It's serious because I have to convince some pretty tough customers to carefully consider parting with their money. That's a lot more challenging than getting them to read blank verse.

Over the past four decades, I've written everything imaginable, from billboards to short films to long books. Some of that stuff may have caused the audience to laugh, cry, ponder, or rage—all important effects, I suppose. But if I can get you to pry open your wallet and spend some cash on a product or service, that is quite an achievement in my book.

Through the years, I've worked in ad agencies and belonged to various professional writing organizations, where I've met a lot of aspiring writers. I've mentored some, too. And I've found that there's one characteristic that all successful writers share in common: They write.

I'm not trying to be funny. I've heard too many wannabes talk about writing, theorize about writing, moan about writing, but they don't actually write, at least not on a daily basis. And that's what it takes to be a professional.

So, if you're sincere about being a really effective copywriter, you must sit down with at least one good idea and write about it for at least an hour a day. Every single day. No excuses. And don't just ramble on. Revise your stuff until you have at least 500 good, solid, publishable words. If you do that long enough, and well enough, one day you will awaken to the fact that you are, indeed, a real pro.

"Because" Copy Is Best Because...

Even if you're not going to become a direct response copywriter, you must master Because copy. Why? Because it's the one writing technique that rewards the audience with a credible promise that's worth believing. It's the payoff for the copy that came before it, and it paves the way for the copy that comes after it. It's the glue that helps the audience stick with your overall message, whether it's short or long. It's a way of respecting the time and attention your audience has given to your communication effort.

Boomers won't tolerate fuzzy generalities. You need to demonstrate that you respect their intelligence each time you communicate with them, and nothing does that more effectively than Because copy that's clear, concise, cogent and creative.

Whether it's done in long form, short bursts or terse bullets, it spells out the benefits for the audience in no uncertain terms. Clarifying a marketing concept or sales proposition—making it truly meaningful—is the heart and soul of Because copy. In essence, it's what great copywriting is all about.

For practical insight into how to write effective Because copy, study ads that have bullet points that go right to the heart of the matter. Appliance and automotive ads can be very instructive for two reasons: 1) some are outstanding, and 2) some are just awful. Read them thoughtfully, and learn to discern the difference.

Great bullet copy is only possible when the copywriter distills each feature/benefit into a clear, concise statement that's meaningful and easy to grasp. Bad bullet copy shoots itself in the foot, because it tends to be self-admiring. It says, "Gee, look at all those features. Aren't they swell?" That kind of copy, which is quite common, is a prime example of the company talking to itself, and although the corporate committee that wrote and approved it might love it, Boomers won't pay it any mind.

Although Because copy is sell copy, it should never sound dull, labored or shrill. To be effective, it has to deftly communicate heavy meaning with a light touch. Good taste and writing skill will help you develop a style that allows you to express complex ideas in a clear, concise way, but it takes lots of practice. In the end, there's no substitute for using just enough of the perfect words to say exactly what you mean. And that takes persistence, patience and a passion for effective communication.

To really grasp the importance of Because copy, read a dozen advertising or marcom headlines that are presumably aimed at Boomers. Try to see things through their eyes and ask: "What's in it for me?" Then do the same with each line of copy. Does the overall thrust of the communication have impact? Does it hit the Boomer where he or she really lives? As a Boomer, do you care about what's being communicated? Are you puzzled by it? Or worse, are you simply bored?

Bottom line: Can you tell what's in it for you?

Do the same exercise with radio commercials, TV commercials, tweets—any form of communication that's knocking on the door of your consciousness.

As you try to see advertising and marcom as the Boomers see them, you'll become increasingly aware of the grammar, vocabulary, sound and feel of effective Because copy. You'll also become aware of how often advertisers miss the mark in terms of reaching and motivating the Boomers they covet.

If you want to see where your brand stands, put your own advertising and marcom to the acid test. Read it as if you were a disinterested Boomer, and be brutally honest. Is there enough Because copy to engage, inform, entertain and motivate you, or are you left wondering,"What's in it for me?" The answers you give will be crucial to your success.

Become A Better Writer Right Now

When asked about the craft of writing, New York sportswriter Red Smith said something to the effect of, "It's really very easy. You just put a piece of blank paper into your typewriter (how very retro), and then you concentrate until little drops of blood appear on your forehead." Although there's no denying that it can be agonizing to face a blank computer screen, it needn't be that painful, if you have a good command of the fundamentals of writing.

All well-educated people should be good writers, but it's often hard to remember all the little things that distinguish the truly capable writer from the dabblers in the craft. Professional communicators simply can't afford to be average writers, that's why we must occasionally take the time to review some of the most important basics of really good writing.

My goal isn't to provide an academic treatise on how to write better. (I hate the sound of snoring.) Instead, I'm just going to cover some ideas that are absolutely, positively guaranteed to instantly transform you into a better writer, if you have the self-discipline to remember and apply them. Real pros will find many of these painfully obvious, but if just one of the tips that follow helps you communicate more effectively, than the review will be worth your time.

The basic goal of all writing is simple: Transfer ideas from one person's mind to another's. If you can accomplish that task, then you're a good enough writer. But that's not good enough when you're trying to communicate with Baby Boomers. To reach them, you have to write clearly, concisely, cogently and creatively. And that's something that few writers can consistently do.

And Boomers won't tolerate communication that lies to them, either intellectually or emotionally. George Orwell wrote that "The great enemy of clear language is insincerity." In other words, if you don't want people to understand what you have to say, state it in a long-winded fashion using lots of fancy words, and they'll walk away scratching their heads. Politicians are masters of this style of lying by omission of meaning. It's underhanded, disgraceful and all too common. Avoid it at all costs, or you'll pay a big price, personally and professionally.

At a minimum, good writers owe the audience two things, clarity and brevity. Write the truth short, sweet and clear as a bell, and you'll hook and hold the reader long enough to communicate your ideas. Write in a long, confusing way, and people will feel cheated, because they won't understand what you're saying, but they will understand that you've wasted their time.

Being consistently clear and concise can be quite a challenge, particularly when you're dealing with a highly complex subject. That's why the ultimate key to success as a writer is relentless revision. Nobody writes a first or second draft so well that it's fit for human consumption. Even the best-selling pros can't do it. James Michener, the author of Hawaii and other epic doorstops, said, "I'm not a very good writer, but I'm an excellent rewriter." And this came from one of America's most successful storytellers.

Of course, clarity and brevity are just minimum standards. To be a really good writer, you must enhance your basic writing skills with techniques that express your unique talent for communication. In other words, you have to be creative.

And, in the end, no matter what you're selling whether it's an ephemeral feeling in a poem or two apples for the price of one, you have to be cogent, because causing others to feel and think and act in a certain way is writing's highest goal.

Reaching that goal with a picky, demanding group like the Baby Boomers can be quite a test, but you'll go a long way toward meeting that challenge when you think like a copywriter.

Perfecting Your Communication Skills

*I*nadvertently letting ageism color your communications isn't the only way to derail the advertising and marcom you create for the Baby Boomer market. You can also damage your brand's image by committing the kind of errors that would disappoint your high school English teacher.

Many of the following tips will seem so basic that you may be offended that I even mention them. And you may be tempted to quickly skip to the next chapter. Don't! Over the past four decades, I've seen these errors made by highly educated, intelligent people who should know better. And, yes, I've committed all of them myself at one time or another.

So before you scoff at the following obvious tips, keep in mind that the one thing that distinguishes the master from the apprentice in any art isn't some arcane, complex knowledge, it's a mastery of the simplest fundamentals. If you're going to create advertising and marcom that influences Baby Boomers, you must be an expert practitioner of the most basic communication skills, many of which we all learned in grade school.

If you believe that you've advanced well beyond the stage where you need to concern yourself with continually perfecting your communication skills, consider this. I was a Kenpo karate black belt instructor for over a quarter of a century. During that time, even the simplest martial arts techniques that I taught students were the same exact ones that I myself drilled day after day, year after year, decade after decade. Whether it's karate or communications, we are all at different points on the same road, so the journey toward perfecting technique can never end. In the final analysis, there is no way to mastery, mastery is the way.

With that in mind, let's consider some tips that are guaranteed to make you a better professional communicator. And at the very least, you'll have a handy reference guide that you can use to hold those who create your communications to an exacting standard.

TIP #1

Never use passive voice

This is the easiest, most reliable quick fix that I can think of. Passive voice is like flypaper. It makes sentences so sticky that the reader's attention gets bogged down. The action slows to a snail's pace, and before you know it, your Boomer is searching elsewhere for something more energizing and engaging.

Active voice is like a powerful engine that sets the sentence in motion and keeps it moving ahead. If you're really serious about being a good communicator, you should create your own personal dictionary made up of active verbs that are so energetic and powerful that they breathe life into every single sentence. This will help you keep your writing—and thinking—more active and productive.

To see what active voice can do for you, carefully edit something that you've recently written, replacing all of the passive verbs with active ones. Then compare the revised version with the original. You'll discover that the revision flows more smoothly and has more energy, and, more importantly, it will be easier to understand.

Example:

Notice how awkward the first sentence seems in comparison to the second.

The songs were sung enthusiastically by the Boomer Tabernacle Choir.

The Boomer Tabernacle Choir sang the songs enthusiastically.

Simple way to improve flow, isn't it? So why do we so often take the passive approach to communication?

TIP #2

Use descriptive nouns

Active verbs are only part of the foundation of good writing. Vivid, meaning-filled nouns are just as important, especially when talking to Boomers, because they value words and ideas that go beyond superficiality. So, thoughtfully select your nouns, taking care to make them concrete and colorful. And start compiling your dictionary of the Most Descriptive Nouns to complement your Active Verb dictionary.

Example:

Chandeliers dotted the ceiling.

The word "chandeliers" in this simple sentence provides a feeling of sparkling elegance and also suggests a vastness of space and large quantity when juxtaposed against the verb "dotted."

TIP #3

Eliminate most adjectives and adverbs

Everybody has heard this time and again, but the fact is that too many writers continue to pile on the adjectives and adverbs until there's so much window dressing that the sentence's idea gets buried. Generally, only puny verbs and lifeless nouns need crutches like adverbs and adjectives, most of which bloat sentences and slow down the train of communication. Keep in mind that Boomers crave sentences that are fit and trim, not wordy and unwieldy. Of course, there are exceptions. A while ago, *Consumer Reports Magazine* painted this vivid picture of Burger King's Chicken Sandwich, using seven adjectives to describe it as a "Moist, springy, peppery piece of oblong pressed chicken on a hefty sesame bun." Sounds almost edible.

TIP #4

Concentrate on communicating ideas

What's the big idea? That's what the busy Baby Boomer is going to ask, so make the subject you're writing about seem brand new, especially if it isn't. The idea is the heart and soul of all communication. If your idea is fresh enough to really get peoples' attention, you've made an important discovery. Dramatize it wisely and well.

Anecdote:

I've had more than a few clients ask me what a big idea is worth. Although I'm not an advocate of smoking, I always cite the case of Marlboro as a paragon of Big Idea branding. What seems to be a rather mundane scenario of a cowboy puffing on a cigarette has created so much marketing mystique (not to mention staying power) that the cash flow the brand generates has built Philip Morris into an international behemoth. That's what a really big idea is worth.

TIP #5

Dramatize each feature with an important benefit

Boomers don't buy products or services, they buy benefits, results, dreams. They don't want to know how swell you think your company or product or service is. They want to know what it's going to do for them. That's why you have to search for the inherent drama in your product or service and bring it to life. Otherwise, you'll lose the Boomer audience, because if you're not talking to their needs, wants and desires, you're talking to yourself.

Example:

Our new toothpaste has extra brighteners.

Extra brighteners in our new toothpaste will make your smile beam.

TIP #6

Use vivid language to paint a lively picture

You can't bore Boomers into remembering what you say. You've got to work to capture and hold their attention. One of the best ways to do this is to paint an unforgettable picture, with carefully chosen words and phrases.Think of your vocabulary as the palette that you'll use to bring your ideas to life. Paint in bright, vivid language, making your ideas so bold that they literally jump off the page and into each Boomer's heart and mind.

I couldn't wait to get to the next sentence after reading this lead in an old *Sports Illustrated*: "Matt Feeney came careening around the corner, his wheelchair tipping perilously as he hurtled toward the finish line." Gimme more. Fast!

TIP #7

Get to the point

Nobody reads Moby-Dick or Lorna Doone anymore unless they absolutely have to for an English Lit class. We live in busy times—an age of instant gratification, where even tweets are beginning to seem a little long-winded. Although Baby Boomers aren't quite as impatient as kids, they still value immediacy in communication, especially in promotional writing. So don't beat around the bush. Cut to the heart of the matter, and make each sentence so interesting and inviting that the Boomer just has to read another. And another. And another. Till you've made your point unmistakably clear.

Example:

The long and short of it. The first example has 34 words, the second, 17. Half the words, all the meaning.

The restaurant was set back from the road approximately 100 feet. There was parking on both sides of the restaurant, and the area set aside for parking was separated by areas of well-kept grass.

The restaurant was set back about 100 feet, with parking on both sides of the well-kept lawn.

TIP #8

Be yourself

Boomers are highly individualistic, so they expect others to be likewise. Besides, what else can you do? You're the creator of your universe of discourse, so let your finest qualities shine through. If humor is your forte, use it well. If you're a logical wizard, use it to your advantage. Whatever your strengths, let your own personal brand of originality put a little extra pizzazz into your writing. Be distinctive. Be creative. Be yourself. That's what style is all about.

However, there are times when you might be called upon to sound like somebody else. That's why you should...

TIP #9

Learn to affect as many different styles as possible

If you're going to reach imaginative Boomers, you have to be a bit of an actor. That's why sometimes you need to be able to write like somebody else. For instance, if your assignment is to recreate Egypt in the 1920s for a travel brochure about a trip to King Tut's digs, you might want to write it with a British accent, so to speak. Or, if you're writing about a thrilling rail tour through Europe, you might want to sound a bit like Agatha Christie. Just remember that the commercial writer is one who writes for the sake of business. That means you're like a craftsman who builds something to the specs stipulated by whomever has hired you. The more artfully you can do that, the more successful you'll be. The best way to learn about affecting various voices is to read a highly diverse selection of writers, and then pick a subject and write about it in several distinctly different styles.

Exercise:

Spend a half hour in the most interesting part of town. After carefully observing the passing scene, write a description of what you saw pretending that you are:

 • a real estate agent

- a cop
- a visitor from China
- a young child
- a Boomer woman
- yourself

To make this exercise even more enlightening and entertaining, relate what you saw in the style of several of your favorite writers. Mine would be Hunter Thompson, Augusten Burroughs, Henry David Thoreau and Walt Whitman. Whom would you choose?

TIP #10

Make your writing bristle with memorability

This is about style with substance. Memorable writing is made up of an important idea wrapped in engaging language. Remember, you can't gain share of market until you gain share of mind. Baby Boomers ignore tons of commercial communications each day. They have to out of simple self-defense. But once you penetrate their apathy, you can carve out a niche—a share of mind—that nothing else can occupy. The best way to accomplish this is to make your writing so interesting, engaging and memorable that Boomers just can't get your ideas out of their heads.

172

Example:

Try to forget the following sentence:

If there were ever a sign that something was terribly wrong in Susan's world, it was never more apparent than the first time she creased her brother's skull with a rusty garden hoe.

TIP #11

Be specific, and don't equivocate

The little truths pave the way for the larger ones. That's why savvy Boomers crave concrete details not fuzzy generalizations. And they want definitive points of view, too. Of course, there's always more than one side to every story, but when you're the writer, it's your obligation to make sure that your take on the subject comes through loud and clear—no ifs, ands or buts. That doesn't mean you can't use understatement now and then. It can be a powerful tool. Just make sure that you don't seem to be teetering on the fence. You just might fall on your face.

Example:

Compare the specificity of the second sentence to the

fuzziness of the first.

As she reached the hill's peak, Emily could see the picturesque town just beyond the bridge.

What does picturesque mean? Probably something different to everyone. This sentence cries out for more detail, as in the following.

Peering over the hill's peak, Emily could see the pink roofs atop white stucco houses rising up from the flat landscape beyond the bridge.

TIP #12
Be accurate and truthful

Being strongly opinionated is one thing. Bending the truth is another. Don't let your creativity cross the line from fact to fiction. McCann-Erickson's motto is "Truth well told," and it's a worthy goal for any communication. Don't try to con Boomers. They're too smart to be fooled, so don't say anything you can't back up with solid facts. Otherwise, you'll get caught in a trap of your own device.

TIP #13

Cut out the jargon, euphemisms and clichés

Sometimes you simply must use words that are unique to a given industry or trade, but the less you do it, the better. Plain-talking Baby Boomers are often so annoyed by jargon that they just tune it out completely. Point missed. And using euphemisms and clichés is not only inappropriate, it's seldom effective. Euphemisms are essentially inaccurate ways to state the truth, and clichés are easy to ignore because they're hackneyed. Instead of falling back on the tried and true (nice cliché, huh?), use fresh language in an interesting, engaging way. Become sensitive to the more subtle aspects of words. Employ nuances of meaning and usage with discrimination. In the final analysis, the challenge is to become a connoisseur of fine language without making your writing stilted.

Exercise:

List a dozen of your favorite clichés, then throw them in the garbage can forever. Then list a dozen of your favorite examples of jargon and do the same.

TIP #14

Choose the proper diction level for the audience

175

All good communication is audience-driven. That means the burden is on you to understand how best to communicate with your readers. There's nothing esoteric about diction. It's simply about choosing the right words for the job. If you're addressing a group of eighth-graders (of any age), set your diction level low, but not insultingly so. If your audience is made up of Baby Boomers, raise the diction level so that it's challenging enough to be interesting and involving, as well as informative. Just remember, it's up to you to capture your audience's attention and hold it. Making conscious choices about diction is one more way to do that.

"Whatever you want to say, there is only one word that will express it; one verb to make it move; one adjective to qualify it. You must seek that word, that verb, and that adjective, and never be satisfied with approximations, never resort to tricks, even clever ones, or to verbal pirouettes to escape the difficulty."

-- Flaubert de Maupassant

TIP #15

Listen to your writing very carefully

The best way to judge writing is to read it aloud. The reason's simple. If it sounds good, then it's going to read well from the Boomer's perspective. If you find yourself tripping over anything, you can be sure that the audience will have even more trouble with it than you do. Good writing must flow smoothly, and the best way to detect any bumps in the road is to listen carefully while you read it out loud.

Exercise:

Choose a recent piece of writing that you're particularly proud of and read it aloud into a recorder while looking into a mirror. After playback, ask yourself if you're still satisfied that it communicates as effectively as possible. Try the same with short passages from your favorite writers.

TIP #16

Simplify. Simplify. Simplify.

This Thoreauvian idea resonates with Baby Boomers because straightforward communication strips away everything that's unnecessary, allowing the simple truth to shine through. Uncomplicated writing isn't unsophisticated; it's powerful, graceful and elegant. So whenever possible, distill the ideas you're trying to communicate to their quintessential meanings.

Exercise:

Take anything that you've written and pare it down to the bone without minimizing any important ideas. With practice, you'll be amazed at how few words you need to clearly and powerfully express the simple essence of an idea.

TIP #17
Be friendly, not phony

It's always helpful to think in terms of the total audience when you're crafting your communication strategy. But when the ink hits the paper, you should be speaking person to person. After all, an audience is made up of individuals, and the best way to address them and their interests is on a first name basis. This is especially important with highly individualistic Baby Boomers, so visualize talking to each of them as if he or she were an old friend. Be warm and open, as well as honest and candid. Write as if you have something important and interesting to say to someone you care about. And above all else, be genuine, because phony stinks like a month old catfish.

Exercise:

Rewrite one of your sales letters or brochures as if you're sharing some great news with your best friend, who happens to be a Boomer.

TIP #18
Write right through Writer's Block

It's true. The fact is that you can overcome this dreaded menace instantly, simply by writing. Write something—anything— as long as it gets your fingers and creative juices flowing again. Once you get rolling, the ideas and words will come. Just remember, if you wait for inspiration, you'll starve to death. So when you feel blocked, ignore it and overcome it by writing.

Exercise:

Next time you feel blocked, get your fingers in gear on the keyboard, and your mind will follow. If you've already written a first draft, type it over, word for word. If you're starting from scratch, write about what you're feeling as you chip away the block. You'll be surprised at how the simple act of typing can trigger the creative writing process.

TIP #19

Search for hidden treasures

Effective brochures and ads need strong, meaningful headlines and subheads. Problem is, great headlines and subheads don't come easily. In fact, you'll usually find the best buried somewhere in the body copy, so don't worry about crafting the perfect head and subhead as you begin writing. However, as you revise, keep a sharp eye out for those few words that express your Big Idea concisely and with flair. You can use them to fashion heads and subheads that directly relate to your Big Idea, and the process will help you sharpen the body copy, as well. Great heads, subheads and copy will keep Boomers involved from the first word to the last, and that's one of the keys to reaching the Boomer Buying Center.

Exercise:

Take a close look at one of your brochures that you're really proud of. Write the main headline and subheads on a piece of paper, then go through the copy very carefully. You'll almost always find words and phrases that you can turn into better headlines or subheads than the ones you actually used.

TIP #20

Ban pleonasm

Pleonasm isn't some exotic disease, it's just a highfalutin' way of saying, Omit words that have no effect on the meaning of the sentence. Lean copy communicates best, so always eliminate extra words. Some of the worst offenders include: "if and when," "unless and until" and "more or less." Those should never be in your writing in any way, shape or form. Oops, sorry about the pleonasm.

Examples:

Here are some less obvious examples of pleonasm. Omit the unnecessary words, then read the sentences aloud. You'll find that shorter is better, and even tiny revisions can make a big difference.

Puddles of water from last night's rain pooled around the house's cracked foundation. (Omit: of water)

Both Mike and Nick went to the party. (Omit: Both)

Cortisone will block the development of further symptoms. (Omit: the development of)

TIP # 21

Remember: "It ain't creative, if it don't sell!"

I once had a client ask me if I'd ever done any "serious" writing. I replied that I'd written countless ads, brochures and commercials that clients had paid quite handsomely for. Of course, the person asking the question was referring to fiction, something that really serious creative writers do when they're not starving to death. Somehow, artistic writing seems more important and prestigious than commercial writing. Nothing could be further from the truth. When you ask a hard-nosed businessperson to buy your writing, and then invest anywhere from thousands to millions of dollars to produce it and run it, that's serious. Sure, artful writing is important. In fact, it's what separates the most effective advertising and marcom from the rest. However, you can't indulge your creative sensibilities unless it helps achieve the goals set by the overall communication strategy, because that's what commercial writing is all about. So just remember, "It ain't creative, if it don't sell."

Exercise:

Take the first page of Moby-Dick, extract the most important ideas that Melville is trying to convey, and rewrite it as if it were a sales letter. This isn't as offbeat as it sounds. All good writers are trying to sell something, even if it's just a point of view or a mood, because that's what keeps people interested and involved enough to keep reading

TIP #22

Read widely and deeply

The best writers are those who love to hang around words. They read novels, how-to books, nonfiction of all kinds, literary magazines, the *National Enquirer* and the backs of cereal boxes. Reading is the best and easiest way to keep in touch with the world of ideas and events, and it exposes you to a wide variety of voices which will help you refine your own stylistic nuances. So when you're not writing, read.

TIP #23

Learn all the rules, then break a few

Make a fetish out of using proper grammar and syntax. And use punctuation with good taste and common sense. Punctuation marks are like traffic signals for your audience. They keep the Baby Boomers' eyes flowing along the communication highway. So be considerate. Tell the reader when to slow down or stop. And above all else, be consistent in the way you use punctuation, especially commas. Then, once you've mastered the rules, feel free to break them occasionally to accomplish your communication goals. Think of this as "special effects" writing.

Exercise:

Take the one piece of writing you're proudest of to a high school English teacher and let him or her put a strict red pencil to it. Then hold onto your ego, because you could be in for a rude awakening. Ask yourself how and why you strayed from the rules you learned in grade school.

TIP #24
Use your thesaurus as often as your dictionary

This sounds so obvious that it borders on being insulting, but I'm continually amazed at how complacent so many writers are about using the first word that comes to mind. You can overcome this indolence by habitually consulting your favorite online dictionary/thesaurus. Consistently referring to these important tools proves that you care about expressing yourself precisely, properly and with panache. And the thesaurus is more than just a spice rack to add a little zest to your writing; it's also a useful brainstorming tool. Simply looking at synonyms and antonyms can reroute your train of thought onto tracks you never imagined.

TIP #25

Write with a powerful voice and unified point of view

Baby Boomers are intelligent, well-educated, discriminating consumers, so your voice should be powerful, and your tone, style and point of view should be consistent from beginning to end. Ditto for the tense of your verbs. If you start out in first person present tense and switch to third person past tense, the reader will have a hard time following the train of your thought, so stay on track. You should also pay close attention to making smooth transitions from sentence to sentence and paragraph to paragraph. When one idea opens the door to the next, the reader has an easier time following the flow, and that's crucial for effective communication.

Exercise:

Rewrite your favorite sales letter or brochure using first, then second, then third person present tense. Notice how the feeling changes with each variation. Then do a version using first person past or future tense. How does that feel? Finally, change all the active verbs to passive, and you'll appreciate how easy it is to turn a powerful piece of writing into a tedious mess.

TIP #26

Research subjects quickly so you can get up to speed instantly

The best writers are quick studies who can ferret out enough important facts about any subject to sound like instant experts in the field. This is a particularly important skill in the fast-paced world of advertising and marketing communications. And with Google, it's never been easier to find all the info you need. In fact, the problem is separating the solid facts from the iffy pretenders. After you've done your instant research, immerse yourself in it. Let those facts fuel your imagination, and you'll begin conjuring up ideas that are surprisingly fresh. If you've got the right stuff, the permutations and combinations of facts, images and feelings will magically come together in some wondrous ways. New ideas will roll out of your head and into your fingers, and you'll write like the wind.

Exercise:

Write a full page of facts about a paperclip. Don't expect this to be easy, and don't be shy about forcing yourself. Creativity is usually more a function of perspiration than inspiration. Now, use your fact sheet to write an ad about paperclips. Make sure the headline dramatizes your Big Idea, then write a paragraph or two of copy that makes people see this humble object in a new and important light. This exercise provides a good way to crystallize your thoughts, and ensure that your writing is clear, concise and direct.

TIP #27
Proofread for perfection

Spelling and punctuation errors are distractions that break the flow of effective communication. As far as proofreading is concerned, there's a simple standard: Perfection. Impossible to achieve, of course, but a worthy goal. Striving for perfection is a matter of good taste. When you let an egregious error slip through, it's like walking around the prom with a piece of toilet paper stuck to the bottom of your shoe. It makes a really lousy impression. Misspellings and the like are almost always the result of laziness and inattention, especially now that a good dictionary is just a click away. (And, of course, you'd be foolish to completely trust spell check. It's too undependable.) In the end, it's your responsibility to get all the little details right. When you do that, it says a great deal about your dedication to the task of precise writing. If you don't bother to seek perfection, don't expect Boomers to rely on what you say. After all, if you can't get the little things right, how can they trust you with bigger things like being accurate and truthful?

Example:

See if this doesn't trip you up.

Four score and sevin years ago.

Hearing it, you'd never know there was a problem; however, reading it causes you to stumble. When that happens, you have to collect your thoughts and start concentrating all over again.

TIP #28

Write

Don't waste time talking about writing, or theorizing about writing or reading about writing. Just write. Every single day. If your goal is to become a better professional communicator, hit the keyboard. Write now!

188

Stop 'Em Dead

*P*laying it safe with advertising and marcom can be dangerous to your business, because the more communication that
floods human consciousness, the less we pay attention. And
in the TwitterNet Age, there's more junk bombarding us with
each passing second.

In this hyperkinetic communication environment, the
ads and marcom that grab and hold an audience are those
that take powerful, well-focused shots directly at the heart of
their target market. When there's a Big Idea in the driver's
seat, these are the ones that will be noticed, remembered and
acted upon. That's why taking creative risks is always more

effective than playing it safe. That's especially true when you're selling to a jaded group like the Baby Boomers.

Successful marketers know just how dangerous safe advertising can be to their bottom line. They realize that everything they do promotionally from TV to tweets has to have Stopping Power. That doesn't mean it shows off or shouts. Instead, it's so thought-provoking and meaningful that it stops Boomers dead in their tracks, compelling them to pay attention.

Effective Stop 'Em Dead ads and marcom always connect with Boomers at the deepest level, the Boomer Buying Center, where all purchasing decisions are made.

To put stopping power into your advertising and marcom, you need to carefully consider the medium you choose, so you can make the most of it. Of course, your ultimate success will depend on how effectively you've used your Big Idea to position your product or service in a uniquely meaningful way. Here are some thought starters.

Print has to have a strong visual stopper that keeps the reader from zipping right past the page. And the graphics must be complemented by a compelling headline followed by well-crafted copy that's just long enough to tell the complete story.

Sounds simple enough, but thumb through the ads in any magazine and prepare to be appalled.

TV is above all else a visual medium. It's easy to determine if a commercial will be effective or not. Just turn off the sound, and if you get the essence of the message, the commercial is a success. Of course, in the Age of Tivo, the visual flow must start dramatically and steadily build to a climax, or it won't hold anyone's attention. The copy should be brief and easy on the ears, and it has to complement rather than parrot the visuals.

Radio is easy if you have a knack for creating theater of the mind. The best radio takes the product or service seriously, but not itself, which is why historically it has used gentle humor to deliver its message. Also believable dialogue that rings true to the ear has far more stopping power than an announcer who mumbles mind-numbing copy points. And there should never be a surplus of gimmicky sound effects or other distractions.

Direct Mail must be engaging, informative and urgent. In addition, it should make a valuable offer that the Boomer finds irresistible. And it must clearly ask for the order without being pushy. This is a difficult medium to shine in, because it's so cluttered, but it can also be a very cost-effective, rewarding way to reach Boomers. Direct marketing techniques are numerous and nuanced. There's even an art and science to designing an effective coupon. That's why it pays to hire a seasoned DM pro who knows when, where and how to use the "tricks of the trade." You'll get your money's worth.

Email marketing is akin to direct mail, but there are more restrictions, and you really do need to heed them. Unless you use permission-based marketing, you'll be labeled a spammer, and you'll be roundly ignored or worse. The powers that be are cracking down on spammers, much to the relief of anyone who uses a computer, so don't just launch junk mail into cyberspace, hoping for the best. Also, it should be obvious that the subject line is where you need to blast your Big Idea, or Boomers will soar right past your email in the blink of an eye.

Social Media, including Twitter, Facebook, et al, can play an important supporting role as long as they're relevant to Boomers. Currently, social media seems to offer fresh opportunities to bond with Boomers, but it's too easy to fall into the trap of trying to create intimacy and ending up looking and feeling like a phony. And as for Twitter, you've got to be a terrific copywriter to tweet 140 characters that form a clear thought that's directly on strategy, as well as meaningful.

Whatever media you employ, you need to make sure your creative executions have real stopping power. In the following chapters, I'll provide step-by-step ways to craft letters, brochures, and direct marketing campaigns that'll help you Stop 'Em Dead. I'll also give you a "preflight" checklist to ensure that all of your advertising and marcom efforts really take off.

For now, though, begin by objectively assessing your latest advertising and marketing communication efforts.Using a critical eye, ask these questions.

- Does this stuff stop me dead?
- If I weren't its creator, would I remember it tomorrow or even later today?
- Does it motivate me to take action now?

If you've answered the above in the affirmative, you're well on the way to getting the job done. If not, you've got some work to do. After all, if your creative executions can't stop you dead, they'll never stop Boomers long enough to get their attention let alone sell them anything.

Letter Perfect

Compared to most advertising and marcom, letters are inexpensive, invaluable sales tools, because they provide the perfect way to talk about whatever you're selling in a personal, engaging and detailed way. Next to a sales call, a letter is the most intimate form of contact you'll ever have with a Baby Boomer. And just as a successful sales call is made person to person, that's how the best letters communicate.

Although a sales letter is a serious business communication, that doesn't mean it should sound cold or technical. Boomers think of themselves as highly individualistic people, not a set of demographic statistics. Communicate like a human being rather than a faceless huckster, and you'll have a real opportunity to promote a personal relationship with Boomers.

Whether you're writing a short, straightforward cover letter or a lengthy, complex sales letter, you must be clear and concise. You must also let your personal warmth come through. Boomers hate insincere phonies, so be honest and human, and they'll listen to your message. Mastering a handful of techniques will go a long way in helping you become letter perfect.

Varying the length of words, sentences, and paragraphs enough to avoid monotony will ensure that the audience isn't lulled to sleep. However, when it comes to overall length, let the subject matter seek its own level. Some still believe that anything over a single page won't get read, especially in the Age of Twitter. That's simply not true. Successful direct marketers have consistently proven that people will keep reading for as long as you can hold their interest. Four, six and even eight-page letters have helped make countless sales. As they age, Boomers become increasingly contemplative, so you can hold their attention at length if you communicate meaningfully.

The longer the letter, the more you'll need an art director's help in creating a pleasing appearance and organizing the flow of copy. The art director will carefully choose the typestyle because a uniquely appealing face (as long as it's big enough and easy to read) is always more inviting than one that's been seen ten thousand times. And because feel is important, the art director will make sure that your paper stock is as substantial as your message. She'll also tastefully use color to help heads, subheads and key points stand out. She may even put a few handwritten comments in color in the letter's margin to reiterate or summarize important points, because that increases reader involvement.

If you decide to act as your own art director (something I'd strongly recommend against), don't cram too many words onto the page. White space gives the reader breathing room, and will make your letter easier to read no matter how long it is. And, of course, underlining and ALL CAPS are definitely out, unless you're intentionally trying to achieve a retro effect or want to scream. Just remember that your goal is to capture and hold the Boomer's attention in a subtle way, not shout at them.

A Letter Is Like A Personal Sales Call

If you want to be letter perfect, you have to pay attention to syntax and grammar, but you also have to be yourself. After all, a sales letter is like a personal sales call, so you've got to let your personality shine through. In the final analysis, strictly following the formal rules of writing isn't as important as making a solid person-to-person connection with your Baby Boomer audience. Just make sure that your diction level matches theirs, so you sound like you're on the same wavelength from beginning to end. Any hint of ageism or condescension will earn your letter a quick trip to the circular file.

Of course, your dominant concern should be to ensure that you communicate your ideas clearly and concisely. That means you avoid jargon whenever possible—big words, too. They might make you feel smart, but they may also alienate the reader, and then everything you've worked to achieve is for naught.

As always, a good way to judge the quality of your writing is to read it aloud in front of a mirror. Listen carefully. Does the entire letter have a lyrical flow? Read it to others—not for content, but to see if they get caught up in the rhythm of the writing. Easy on the ears is gentle on the mind.

When you're finally satisfied with the tone and content, put the letter aside for a day or two. You'll forget about it, but your subconscious won't. When you come back to it, you might be surprised at how much fine-tuning needs to be done. At this point, a real pro will rewrite it at least three times, and that's a bare minimum.

When it comes to style, don't even think about it, because your writing will become affected. Style is simply the unique way that you express yourself. Just say whatever needs saying, and your style will come through. Don't try too hard, though, because it's easy to let your ego get carried away, and then your "artistry" might bury your message. Keep in mind that you don't need to dazzle your audience with your wordsmithing; before anything else, you owe them clarity and brevity.

If you're really serious about becoming letter perfect, start reading every single letter that comes across your desk. Study each carefully. Put the lousy ones in one file, the good ones in another. (If you have trouble deciding if a letter is good or bad, it's bad.) Every Friday afternoon, study your collection. Analyze why the good ones work and why the bad ones don't. Over the long run this exercise will make you a better letter writer. Guaranteed.

P.S. Research has consistently shown that almost everybody reads a P.S., so remember to include one that sums up your Big Idea. In this case, it's that it takes practice, practice and more practice to become letter perfect.

12 Ways To Make Yourself Perfectly Clear

Becoming a writer is a lifelong process. You're never really finished perfecting your craft, especially when it comes to being clear about exactly what you're saying. Crystal clarity is essential if you're trying to communicate with Baby Boomers. They're well educated, sophisticated and demanding consumers who will simply ignore any piece of communication that's obtuse.

If you've been regularly writing your own sales letters, you're probably a pretty good writer by now, so I'm going to share some things that you must master to become even better. If you keep these tips in mind, you'll be able to polish the rough edges until everything you write is crystal clear. If you think this smacks of trying too hard, you'll never be an accomplished professional.

Striving for absolute clarity is the minimum that a good professional writer owes his or her audience. This should be painfully obvious, but it's not. Don't take my word for it. Skim the first page of a dozen or so books at random. Better yet, try to decipher just about any written communication from the government—you'll need the Rosetta Stone to penetrate the meaning. Ironically, the government is supposed to be our friend. Of course, that isn't always the case. Consider the exalted civil servant who said, "Let me make one thing perfectly clear," as he desperately labored to obfuscate the obvious.

Problems of clarity generally arise from two sources. The first is a brew of ineptitude, carelessness and laziness. The second source is that certain writers want to pretend that they're communicating something of substance, when all they really want to do is give the appearance of communication. And that, unfortunately, often seems to hold true in advertising and marketing communications, where playing it fast and loose with the truth seems to be business as usual.

The best copywriters know that nothing speaks as clearly or loudly as the truth well told. No thinking person will tolerate anyone who willfully distorts the facts, and no one is going to buy anything from anyone who treats them like a fool.

People feel cheated when they don't have a clear grasp of exactly what you mean after having read what you've written, because you've wasted their time. If you don't approach the creation of your sales letters with crystal clarity in mind, you're not going to ring up too many sales with Boomers.

"Buy something from you? I'm not even sure what you said!" is the way they'll react to poorly written promotional materials of any kind. This is especially true of letters, which by their very nature, have a more personal feel than other types of marcom.

So, if your goal is to have Boomers really understand what you're talking about, consider these tips, and you will clearly be on the road to becoming a more powerfully effective writer.

1. **Keep it simple.** Simplicity is key to clear communication.

2. **Eliminate jargon, euphemisms and clichés.** Use fresh language in an interesting and engaging way. Become sensitive to the subtle aspects of vocabulary and diction. Employ nuances of meaning and usage with fine discrimination.

3. **Play by the rules.** Use proper syntax and grammar. You must master writing by the rules before you can even consider breaking them.

4. **Choose powerful verbs** to drive each sentence. Forget

about passive voice, keep it active, and you'll seldom have to worry about using adverbs to shore up weak-sounding verbs.

5. **Thoughtfully select nouns.** Make them concrete and colorful. A sure sign of a poor writer is the tendency to lean on adjectives to help support puny nouns. And don't use nouns as verbs. "Impact" is primarily a noun. Sure, you can use it as a verb, but when you do, it feels like jargon. Besides, it's not nearly as clear or powerful as the word "strike," for instance. And use your thesaurus liberally, because that's where all the really cool words hang out. In fact, you should think of the thesaurus as a spice rack that can add a little zing to your writing and keep people interested enough to continue reading.

6. **Cut back on adjectives and adverbs.** If you use descriptive nouns and active verbs you won't need to embellish your writing with too many adjectives and adverbs. And that will be just fine, because more often than not, they simply bloat sentences and get in the reader's way.

7. **Learn to spell.** Don't laugh. There are too many examples of this flaw, especially in an age when email and Twitter

have encouraged people to get downright sloppy about spelling, not to mention syntax and grammar. Correct spelling shows that you care about your writing and have enough self-respect to use a dictionary when in doubt. Readers are sure to trip over a word that's mispelled (see what I mean?), because it sticks out like a sore thumb, and that's guaranteed to derail the communication process. And, of course, don't ever fully trust Spell Check in Word or any other program. The only proofreader you can rely on is yourself.

8. **Listen to your writing.** The ear loves clarity the way the nose loves freshly baked bread. Read your writing out loud so you can hear it flow. If it doesn't sound good to you, it's certainly not going to sound good to the reader. Elegantly rhythmic writing makes it easier for the reader to embrace and absorb what you're trying to communicate. Be sure to choose your words and sentence construction with a tasteful ear so your writing really sings.

9. **Give the reader concrete details**. Your writing will always seem more real and less abstract when you engage and enliven the senses. Let the reader smell, feel, see, hear

and touch exactly what you are talking about. Don't go overboard, though; a little of this goes a long way. Keep in mind that specifics are much clearer than generalities, and they give your writing more credibility, too.

10. **Learn to cut without bleeding.** It seems like the writer with the least to say often uses the most words to say it. But if you're going to write like a pro, you have to be your own most ruthless editor. It's easy to fall in love with your own words, but too many unnecessary ones just clutter the landscape and get in the way of what you're writing about. Just remember that you're conveying ideas not words, so make sure your writing gets directly to the point and stays there. Here's a good rule of thumb: If it doesn't move the Big Idea forward, cut it. Period.

11. **Use punctuation with good taste.** Punctuation marks are like traffic signals that keep the reader's eyes and thoughts flowing along the highways, side streets and back roads of your writing. Whatever you're writing about is likely to be unexplored territory for your audience, so be considerate. Tell the reader when to slow down or stop. And be consistent in the way you use punctuation—

especially commas.

12. **Maintain a unified point of view and voice.** An orderly, logical flow paves the way for clarity, so once you get on track, stay there from start to finish. Your tone, style, and the tense of your verbs should also be consistent from beginning to end, unless you have a compelling reason to vary them. And your transitions from one sentence to the next and one paragraph to another should be logically consistent, as well.

Ultimately, there are no shortcuts to becoming a crystal clear writer. Use the tips I've given you as a starting point and do a lot more homework on your own. Then write and rewrite until everything you want to communicate is stated so perfectly that it's simple, straightforward and easy to understand.

Is that clear?

Hit The Bull's-Eye:
10 Steps To Creating
A Direct Marketing
Campaign That Works

*H*ow would you like to be welcomed into the home of your Ideal Baby Boomer—the one person who's the best possible prospect for your product or service—and be able to put your most convincing sales message right under his or her nose? Well, that's what direct marketing is all about—hitting the bull's-eye.

Direct marketing, of course, includes much more than just direct mail, although that's an important element in many DM campaigns. But no matter what the medium, the basics are the same: Clearly identify your Ideal Boomer in as much detail as possible, craft the most cogent sales message for that person, then deliver that message in such an engaging and meaningful way that it simply can't be ignored.

Your Ideal Baby Boomer can be defined by a set of very specific demographic and psychosocial characteristics. Once you've identified those, you'll know that your Ideal Boomer has certain values and beliefs that are of paramount importance, a certain educational background and a certain house on a certain block. Your Ideal Boomer will also live a certain lifestyle, share certain interests with a certain circle of family and friends, and have a certain income, as well as certain buying habits. The possibilities are endless, but the more certain you can be about those variables, the better you'll know your Ideal Boomer, and the better you'll be able to sell to him or her.

It's challenging but rewarding, because when you transform your Ideal Boomer into a customer, he or she will likely remain loyal to your business as long as you deliver as promised. That's one of the distinct advantages of direct marketing. In a world where brand loyalties are vanishing, the DM customer tends to buy from the same trusted companies again and again. This loyalty is also the reason that the best list of prospects you'll ever have is your own house list of satisfied customers.

Of course, DM is such a highly sophisticated and diverse discipline that I can only scratch the surface here. But if you're interested in using DM to build sales as well as your brand image, here's a bare-bones overview of the steps you should take.

Although many of the points have already been covered earlier in this book, the following puts a summary of what you need to know right at your fingertips.

1. Seriously consider hiring an experienced DM expert you can call on for advice as you craft your campaign from concept through execution and fulfillment. You may want to cut corners and do it all yourself, but a consultant can save you a great deal of time and money, not to mention frustration, by helping you avoid obvious missteps.

2. Identify your Ideal Boomer as clearly and completely as possible.

3. Buy a list of those Ideal Boomers from a reputable list broker, or create the list yourself.

4. Decide on a valuable offer. The offer is the heart of any

DM effort and must be carefully thought through and clearly stated. Dollars-off tied to an Act Now! command is an obvious and common tactic, and multiple offers for different purchase levels can also be effective.

5. Keep close tabs on sales results and other statistical measures of your campaign. Set up a system that tracks effectiveness as well as cost efficiency.

6. As you gather data and tabulate results, begin building your house list for your next DM effort.

7. Don't skimp on frequency. You can never count on a single execution to help you meet your communication or sales goals. If you're doing a direct mail campaign, mail often—at least once a month for six consecutive months—more frequently, if you have the budget.

8. At the end of the campaign's run, analyze the overall results.

9. Based on those results, refine your executions, eliminating the negatives and strengthening the positives. Do A/B

splits to determine more effective ways to communicate your sales message.

10. Repeat steps 2 through 9.

The best thing about DM is that it talks back to you. You'll quickly know if it's working or not simply by checking your sales results against dollars invested.

DM can also:
- Be used to build your company's image, as well as its sales.
- Be used as a research tool to measure the effectiveness of your offer and copy by comparing the results of A/B split mailings (provided the samples are large enough.)
- Yield marketing information that will help you build a solid house list, as well as more refined creative executions.
- Facilitate immediate, direct interaction with your Ideal Boomer.

The bottom line is that using DM techniques will give you

the best chance of hitting your Ideal Boomer right in the bull's-eye—that elusive Boomer Buying Center, where all sales begin.

20 Steps To Creating
A Hardworking Brochure

A brochure is like a silent salesperson that speaks volumes about your company, as well as its products and services. Effective brochures can be excellent sales tools when you're courting the Baby Boomer market because they give you a chance to tell your brand story in an expansive, engaging way. So here's a step-by-step guide that will help ensure that your next brochure looks and sounds like your star salesperson.

Once again, although many of the points have already been covered earlier in this book, what follows puts a convenient recipe for success right at your fingertips.

1. Carefully consider the fundamental nature of your

product or service. On an emotional level, what are you really selling? What are the most important features and benefits? Why should Boomers consider buying what you're selling? What's the Big Idea? How do you use that Big Idea to create a unique position that will carve out a niche in Boomers' minds? Don't go beyond this step until you've nailed down definitive answers in writing.

2. Pinpoint your market. Identify your Ideal Baby Boomer as specifically as possible, demographically, psychographically and spiritually. Clearly specify every fact you can that will help make this abstraction closely resemble a living, breathing person.

3. Study the brochure environment, especially "junk" mail. Every day your competition pours into mailboxes around the world. Each brochure adds to the clutter, overwhelming Boomers and discouraging them from reading all but the most urgent and important ones. Ask yourself: Why should I read any of these? Why do I find it so easy to throw away almost every single brochure after barely a glance? What can I do to help ensure that my brochure will get noticed and be a keeper?

4. Refine your basic selling concept. Exactly what does your Big Idea promise your Ideal Boomer? How can you back up that promise with credible evidence? Your basic selling concept will serve as the guiding light for the entire brochure so make it clear, concise, cogent and creative.

5. In direct marketing, the offer is the heart of the effort. It must be presented in a way that makes it seem as important and valuable as it actually is.

6. Limit the offer. People respond to deadlines, so set a realistic one.

7. Guarantee your products and services in a way that minimizes risk. This is essential when selling to value-oriented Boomers who hate taking chances. Give them a 30-day free trial backed by a full money-back guarantee. If you can make a stronger guarantee, like double your money back, that's even better. If you really believe in the value of what you're selling, show it in no uncertain terms.

8. Make it easy to respond to the offer. You can increase

response by including a postpaid BRC, having a toll-free number and secure website, and encouraging small monthly payments by credit card. Anything that facilitates the sale will help build a bigger bottom line.

9. Make your claims credible. Claims that can't be cogently supported aren't very convincing. Use testimonials (with pictures), quote research results, cite anything that makes what you say believable.

10. Consider content before design. Dramatic, compelling graphics can stop Boomers dead in their tracks, but ultimately words sell. So, figure out what you're going to say and how you're going to say it before you consider the look and feel of the brochure.

11. Design should flow from your Big Idea. Graphics must complement what you say and support your basic selling concept. Be flexible, though. Don't tie your designer's hands. Instead, encourage him to create the best possible graphic expression of your basic selling concept. And don't use stock photography. Sure, it's a lot cheaper than hiring a pro for a custom shoot, but if you use stock, its

almost certain to show up in your competitors' executions, and you'll end up looking like one of the herd rather than a leader.

12. Unless your staff has the experience and expertise to do an outstanding job, hire pros to execute the copy and design. Taking a DIY approach to creative executions can be as tacky as reproducing your brochure on a color copier rather than using a top-flight printer. Amateur efforts may save a few bucks, but they'll damage your brand image.

13. Speak person to person. Each of your brochures will be talking to a single Ideal Boomer not the sub-segment of some faceless market, so treat that person like an intelligent individual who doesn't like to waste time or money. And avoid using jargon, buzz words and other annoyances that turn off Boomers.

14. Never state a feature without stating its benefit. Boomers want to know "what's in it for me?" If you can't state a genuine benefit for a given feature, don't mention it at all
.

15. Offer a free gift. Boomers love freebies, so this is an

effective way to increase involvement in your messaging and response to your offer. Emphasize the free gift several times, and consider offering multiple gifts tied to different purchase levels.

16. Make friends with a good printer. Print production is where a good chunk of your budget will be going, so know thy printer. Have him or her explain the economies of various sizes and formats. Find out what die-cutting, embossing, and hot-stamping cost before they're designed into your piece. Make full-sized dummies of the brochure with the paper you're thinking of using. Do everything possible to catch problems early, because once your brochure is on the press, changes will be very costly. And be sure to be present to check and maintain quality as the press rolls.

17. To color or not to color. Research suggests that 4-color printing (especially bleed) increases the response rate while other uses of color (2/C, for instance) don't. So, if you can pop for the extra money, go with full-color bleed.

18. After you've identified your Ideal Boomer as precisely

as possible, have a long talk with a mailing list broker. This person can help you rent the most effective, efficient list possible. Keep in mind, however, that a purchased list will never be as good as your own house list, so start building it from day one.

19. Introduce yourself to the local postmaster. This person can be an invaluable resource that's often overlooked. I've never met a postmaster who wasn't friendly, helpful and eager to share his or her knowledge about how to get the most from the postal system. And, of course, you'll need a bulk mailing permit and an open account with a balance sufficient to cover any cost overruns.

20. Build a better winner. After a successful mailing, there's an understandable tendency to keep running the same brochure, but you can increase your response rate over time by doing some simple in-house research. Run an A/B split mailing with A, the winner you've been running, as the control and B, the pretender to the throne. Vary B by putting a new spin on an old offer, adding a more valuable offer, or by trying a new response mechanism. You can also vary headline and copy. Change only

one thing at a time, though, so you can clearly understand the cause of any differences that might occur. Then mail A to half your list and B to the rest. Compare results, and you'll either have a greater appreciation for your old execution or a new winner to beat.

The key to creating a brochure that works as hard as you do is to keep experimenting and learning. Over time you'll find that success comes more easily when you know and use all of the little edges that make up the art and science of building a better brochure.

The Creative Checklist
40 Steps To Creating More Effective Advertising And Marcom

*T*his book has covered many topics related to the creative execution of advertising and marketing communications aimed at Baby Boomers. To give you a handy reference guide, this chapter will summarize some of the most important points in the form of a checklist.

Use this Creative Checklist as a kind of preflight routine to help ensure that your marcom takes off with full power and makes a smooth landing in the marketplace.

I've tried to put the steps in logical order, but if some seem out of sync, please trust that I had a good reason for grouping things the way that I did. So, here are forty ways to make your advertising and marcom more effective when you're trying to reach the Boomer market.

1. A Big Idea is more important than big words and bigger pictures. Make sure you've based your communication on a compelling, cogent concept.

2. Ask, "Who's my Ideal Boomer—the one most likely to buy my products and services?" Define him or her as precisely as possible, so you can talk to that individual in a direct and personal way.

3. Why will my Ideal Boomer benefit from my product or service? After you've identified that person, clearly state the exact benefits you can offer him or her.

4. How will my Ideal Boomer benefit from my product or service? Dramatize the psychosocial benefits that person will enjoy by buying whatever you're selling.

5. Make the main appeal emotional. Don't just tell your Ideal Boomer how great the features of your product or service are; tell him or her how good they're going to feel

about themselves and their futures after they buy.

6. Give your Ideal Boomer a good excuse to buy. Most people won't admit to buying something simply for emotional reasons. That would seem irrational, so give them lots of rational reasons they can use to support their buying decision.

7. Make your appeal timely. You can always make your product or service seem perfect for the times, if you're creative. Measure the impact of your communication in terms of contemporary economic and social trends.

8. Display good taste. Think of your marcom as your top salesperson. You wouldn't dream of letting a representative of your company present himself in a less than professional way, and you should hold your marcom to the same high standard. Be especially cautious when using humor. Only a handful of professional writers can pull it off well, so it's wise to be satisfied with a sincere, straightforward presentation of the facts. McCann-Erickson has a timeless motto that sums up what tasteful advertising and marcom should be all about: Truth well told.

9. Forget about your product or service. People don't want things, they want results and benefits. Women don't buy dishwashing liquid because they like it, they buy softer hands and cleaner plates. Photographers don't buy cameras, they buy a way to document and preserve treasured memories.

10. Give your Ideal Boomer a clear, concise picture of exactly what you're trying to sell. It's OK if beauty shots and a big logo dominate your advertising and marcom, but they must be set in the context of an overall execution that's interesting, engaging, and relevant, or you can ring up No Sale.

11. Illustrate your main selling proposition. A picture may not always be worth a thousand words, but it can be worth a lot of sales. Sometimes what you show and how you show it sells more effectively than what you say. Words alone can't always achieve your goals. I know that some successful direct marketers will take exception with this, but DM needs to make better use of inspired, meaningful art direction.

12. Getting attention is not an end in itself. If you create an execution that captures everybody's attention for the wrong reasons, you won't make many sales. Besides, you don't really want everyone's attention do you? Wouldn't you be satisfied with the undivided attention of your Ideal Boomer? And keep in mind that attention is a lot easier to get than serious prospects. So beware. If you try to be a little too clever, or a bit irreverent, or a shade tasteless, you'll get noticed, but you may also get a lot less than you bargained for in terms of sales.

13. Communicate quickly. Headlines and subheads must get directly to the heart of the matter without mincing words. Being direct will help convert browsers into interested, involved prospects, and some of them will become buyers.

14. Make your headlines sound newsworthy, original, and distinctive. If you don't grab your Ideal Boomer with the headline, you're dead in the water, so take your time before settling on one. You should have at least a dozen good alternatives to consider. And make sure that each is conceptually linked to your Big Idea.

15. Be positive. The psychological distance from a negative thought to positive benefits is often too great a leap to make, so a negative headline has to be extraordinary to work as well as a positive one.

16. The headline must clearly address your Ideal Boomer's self-interest. Well-written copy will keep people reading until they eventually become involved with the benefits of your product or service—the "what's in it for me" part of the execution that everyone looks for.

17. Design the copy to gently lead your Ideal Boomer to the sale. Get the reader nodding in agreement from the very first word of copy to the very last, and the final Yes that makes the purchasing decision will come more easily.

18. Don't overinflate claims. A solid, credible piece of copy built on believable, factual statements is always preferable to pure puffery. But you still have to be creative in the way that you serve up the hard facts.

19. Be picky about your diction. Carefully choose your words and the way you use them. Make sure that your

vocabulary sets a tone that's open, honest, sincere and personal. Keep one eye on your copy and one on your dictionary. And use your thesaurus often, because that's the garden where the most beautiful and meaningful words grow.

20. Use bright language. Keep your copy vivid and filled with action. Minimize adjectives and adverbs, maximize descriptive nouns and powerful verbs. Choose your words wisely, and your writing will shine with eloquence, power and memorability.

21. Explain what needs to be explained. Tell your Ideal Boomer exactly what he or she needs to know. But never be condescending. After all, when was the last time you bought something from someone who made you feel inferior?

22. Don't argue with your Ideal Boomer. Make your points with logic, reason, emotion, whatever seems most appropriate, but do it deftly and politely. If you become argumentative, you've lost the sale. After all, when was the last time you bought something from someone who

made you angry?

23. Be specific. Don't let your copy get lazy or sloppy. People will generally forgive errors of the spoken word, but their expectations rise dramatically when it comes to the written word. Amateurish writing speaks for itself— quite loudly. And don't think that you'll be able to get by with florid language. That won't increase your sales, it will just make you sound Victorian. Be concise and specific as you write copy, and Boomers will reward you with their attentiveness.

24. Tell Boomers exactly what you want them to do. Don't beat them over the head with it, but don't beat around the bush either. Just clearly and directly tell them what kind of action they should take.

25. Ask for the order. Do you really have to consider this obvious point? Well, from the looks of too much marcom, I'm afraid so. But use good judgment in this touchy area. You can even be subtle, but by all means tell them to buy now!

26. Repeat your Big Idea in different ways, so your Ideal Boomer can reflect on every facet of it. With a little creativity, you can articulate your main selling proposition many times over without sounding repetitive.

27. Keep your writing simple. If your copy is too hard to understand—if a person of average intelligence and education can't fathom it—you'll never make the sale. So, beware of tech talk, industry jargon, lofty diction and "impressive" words. Remember that complexity baffles, simplicity sells.

28. Be accurate and truthful. If you overstate your case, people will turn you off, so don't say anything you can't back up with facts and feelings that resonate as the truth.

29. Hire a graphic artist. You'll find that the creative expertise and good taste of an experienced, professional art director can make even ordinary marcom seem almost extraordinary.

30. Visually illustrate the inherent drama in your product. This will take some creative exploration, but it's well

worth the time and expense. When you graphically dramatize your product's Big Idea, it becomes more lifelike for your audience.

31. Look at the layout very carefully. Remember that the eye is built for motion. Does it easily flow from one element to the next without hopping, skipping and jumping around?

32. Variety is the spice of eyes. Conversely, bore the eyes, and you bore the person, and bored people don't buy. Unlike copy, where simplicity is a virtue, in art direction, a little visual complexity can be interesting and engaging as long as it supports rather than distracts from the Big Idea.

33. Can you read the typeface easily? Don't laugh, the only reason you can't remember ever seeing an ad with an unattractive typeface is that you didn't bother to read it. And don't cram the ad with so much copy that the type has to be tiny. This is especially important when selling to Baby Boomers. Squinters seldom become buyers.

34. Keep sentences short. Paragraphs, too.

35. Will it play in Peoria? That's the kind of place where most people live, so don't put all your money behind the latest fads and fashions in advertising and marcom. They may play in New York and LA, but they may not hit your Ideal Boomers where they really live.

36. Don't get too artsy. Sure, creativity is important, but the Big Idea is the star of the show, so don't overwhelm it with a lot of window dressing. To make your product or service really stands out, avoid affectation and create a look that emphasizes your Big Idea.

37. Keep the layout active. Just as passive voice makes for weak writing, passive visuals make for weak marcom. Show your product in use. Bring your service to life. Make it dynamic, exciting and interesting. And, unless you have a very compelling reason, when you show people, make them appear active not posed.

38. Trust your creative instincts. They're there, just get in touch with them. Even if you don't communicate with your creative side too often, you can discover it, nurture it and put it to work in your advertising and marcom, if

you try. So, trust your creativity. Gamble a little. Play a hunch here and there. Cut loose, and give it your best shot. The only thing you have to lose is your inhibitions.

39. Keep trying. Some of the most hard-hitting, effective executions in history have yet to be created. So let the pioneer spirit guide you. Do your best, and even if you don't create the world's greatest marcom, you'll sell a lot more products and services.

40. Remember, it ain't creative, if it don't sell. Ultimately for marcom of any kind, the bottom line is all that really counts. Making the sale is of paramount importance; everything else is secondary at best. If the cash register doesn't ring, the marcom wasn't worth the time, effort or money it took to create it.

The above checklist should help you assess where your current advertising and marcom are right now, as well as where your future efforts should be headed. Just keep in mind that there are no easy answers or formulas you can use when you're pursuing a group of picky prospects like the Baby Boomers. It takes intelligent planning and focused effort to create communications that work with these demanding and savvy consumers. That's why it always pays to take a really close look at every little detail before you roll out your next execution or campaign. In the end, everything you put out in the marketplace should sound like your star salesperson, so make it really shine.

The Beginning:

Listen For The Boom!

*I*f your company is like most, you haven't really started to pursue the burgeoning Baby Boomer market. In fact, you probably haven't even considered how to listen to and effectively communicate with this highly individualistic, iconoclastic group until now. That's why you're only at the beginning of what may be a long and profitable journey. The good news is that you're not alone. The vast majority of companies, especially in consumer products, continue to overlook this lucrative target market.

That's a huge error because The Boomers are the biggest,

most important group of consumers for almost any market segment you can name, including high-tech. They may not be early adapters, but when they become enthusiastic about a product, they tend to buy for their kids and grandkids, as well as themselves.

Considering how much more ready cash they have than Gen Xers and Yers, it's a real mystery why so few advertising dollars are specifically allocated to reach the Boomer market. Maybe it's simply prejudice born of ageism—the fact that almost every young American seems uncomfortable with the realities of growing older. Or, maybe it's because marketers don't really appreciate the fact that Boomers have always enjoyed being on the cutting edge—that they actually like to try new brands and innovative technology.

For example, despite what many marketers believe, Boomers are the most plugged-in generation in history. Recent statistics reveal that Boomers spend over 9½ hours watching some form of video every single day. That's more than any other market segment. In fact, they make up 1/3 of all TV, online, social media and Twitter users. And they're also highly likely to have broadband connections.

Although they dominate 1,023 out of 1,083 consumer packaged goods categories, marketers still act like Boomers aren't worthy of distinctive advertising and marcom initiatives that speak directly to their special interests, needs and desires. If they fully appreciated the potential profitable sales the Boomers represent, more companies would custom-tailor creative marketing programs that hit the very heart of this highly sophisticated group of consumers.

It's as if these companies believe that the Boomers are suddenly going to abandon the Consumer Culture that they themselves helped create. That's a big mistake, because Boomers are going to continue to consume at a very healthy rate until the day the entire generation drops dead. And they are going to do all that consuming in better health than previous generations, so they'll be an enormous economic force for decades to come.

This will happen despite the fact that Boomers' retirement funds have been trashed by the recent lousy economy. But adversity is nothing new to the Boomers, so they aren't about to wilt down the home stretch of their lives. After all, they've thrived in the face of severe economic downturns that have lasted for years at a time during every decade since the '60s.

Through it all, the Boomers have continued spending, and today they're still the largest, most affluent generation in world history. If the Boomers have proven anything, it's that when it comes to spending, you can never count them out. That's why right now is the best time to prepare to profit from the coming Boom! Companies that learn how to successfully woo this high net worth market should enjoy lots of incremental profits for years to come.

As you begin, though, keep in mind that Boomers are demanding, quirky and picky. They need to be communicated with in ways that are up to their high standards, even if they can't clearly define what those are. As this book has suggested, if you learn how to speak with them in direct, honest and open ways, you'll be welcomed into the Boomer Buying Center, the place where all sales begin. So what are you waiting for? Start today and listen for the Boom.

Food For Thought

Learning to meaningfully communicate with Boomers is more art than science. Much more.

While solid research findings will unquestionably help you understand Boomers, translating those insights into creative messages that resonate with this fickle group is an intuitive art, not a scientific puzzle that some quant can solve.

The rest of this chapter will cover disparate ideas for you to contemplate as you begin to decide exactly where and how your business can best position itself against the Boomer market.

These thought starters will help you begin to understand and appreciate the unique spirit of this lively group of consumers. Toss off your preconceived notions and immerse yourself in what follows, and soon you'll begin to think of creative strategies and tactics that you can use to encourage Boomers to open their hearts and wallets to your products and services.

101 Thought Starters

Many of the following thought starters have been intentionally placed in random order to help you break out of conventional constraints and linear thinking and get in touch with your creativity. The exceptions, like references to specific counseling techniques or philosophical concepts, are in sequence for the sake of clarity.

It's not necessary (or even desirable) for you to read straight through these tidbits. Instead, immerse yourself in them a little at a time. Contemplate each one, letting it really soak into your subconscious. It may well be that only one of these ideas will stimulate your creative impulses. But that will make it all worthwhile, because once unleashed, your creativity will suggest many ways that you can help put the Boom! in your bottom line. So here goes...

1. If you believe the latest statistical approach to marcom will resonate more deeply with Baby Boomers than insightful creative communications, keep in mind that the Boomers came of age during the artistic renaissance of the 1960s. That cultural revolution was born of the Boomers' discontent with the status quo and fueled by their creativity. Ultimately, it was their penchant for creative exploration and experimentation that motivated them to seek more authentic and meaningful ways of living.

2. Boomers comprise the single most vibrant and exhilarating consumer group in the history of the world, so don't fantasize that you can somehow bore them into buying your products and services. You've got to tickle them in just the right way, and then you have to communicate your brand story clearly, concisely, creatively and cogently.

3. There are no hard and fast rules you can apply to marketing to Boomers, but there are effective ways to approach

them. Discover and follow those ways with insight and sensitivity, and you'll succeed where others fail.

4. The Boomers are driven by an innovative verve that has always motivated them to try new things and new ways. In the '60s, they experimented with sex and drugs. Today, they're opening themselves up to new lifestyles, adventurous travel expeditions and continuing education for fun and profit. What new challenges will they take on next? Answer that question with your products and services, and you'll be in for quite a ride.

5. The Boomers spawned America's Culture of Youth, but psychosocially, they moved on long ago. Given their history of rebellion and civil disobedience, you can be certain that they won't placidly accept the humiliations and affronts to dignity that typify the ageist tendencies in today's society. In fact, ageist attitudes and behaviors will change radically over the next decade. Why? Because if money talks, the Boomers are about to embark on an unprecedented gabfest.

6. Historically, the sheer massive number of Boomers has

amped up the economic importance of every common experience that they've ever shared. As they've passed through various developmental stages, the Boomers have created and defined markets, many of which withered and died when this lucrative juggernaut passed on to the next stage. Every step of the way, whatever the Boomers focused on has become a dominant force, socially, politically and economically. It pays to remember that the Boomers don't often respond to marketer-made consumer trends; instead they create and transform trends. Examples of this abound at home and at work, as well as in the marketplace. All have become increasingly democratized thanks to various Boomer social initiatives, including the Women's Movement. Along the way, the Boomers have also radically revolutionized the food and fashion industries, among others. The bottom line is that truly visionary captains of industry have learned to listen to and follow the real muscle that drives America's economic engine: the Baby Boomers.

7. Marketing is all about creating ways to attract and hold the interest of complex minds and persuading them to take specific actions. However, over the past few decades,

marketing has grown increasingly numbers-oriented. In a corporate sense, taking a scientific approach to marcom may feel safer and more certain than purely creative approaches, but that ignores the fact that it's impossible to quantify the power of creativity. Think about the world's most popular brands. The most successful are those that have a Big Idea that resonates so deeply that it owns a share of countless minds. Ultimately, that large share of minds leads to a large share of market. Those Big Ideas aren't the products of juggling numbers. They're the creations of fearless thinkers who understood that powerful ideas have their roots in courageous risk taking rather than the shelter of an uninspired numbers game.

8. In younger age cohorts, brand choice is largely influenced by peers. That makes things much simpler for market-ers, because they can just go with the flow of whatever is fashionable at the moment. Boomer buying behavior is much more difficult to influence. Although peers can sway each other in any cohort, Boomers are very indi-vidualistic and independent. Early on, they emotionally liberated themselves from the herd instinct, so their range of choices is much more diverse. Marcom quants would

have you believe that their theories and methods can be applied to any age cohort, but genuine freedom of choice makes predicting Boomer behavior on a macro scale very dicey at best. That's why it's wisest to treat each Boomer as a Market Segment Of One.

9. If you can get in touch with and unleash your own personal brand of creativity, you'll discover ways to tempt Boomers to soar toward your brands on flights of their own imaginations.

10. Creativity is never nice and neat, so learn to live with the ambiguity and anxiety that inevitably accompany it.

11. Developmental psychology offers a treasure trove of empirically-tested theories that can help guide your understanding of Baby Boomers. But don't depend on others to do your homework for you. Do you own research, and it will sink into your subconscious, enhancing your creativity. And remember, the most important insights can't be empirically derived, so after you've done your homework, trust your intuition.

12. Quit being so product-centric in your marcom. Boomers don't care about features; instead, they focus on their feelings. It's your job to determine how to evoke positive feelings about your product and harness the power of the emotions that result. Figure that out, and you'll be well-received in the Boomer Buying Center.

13. Economics and marketing are social sciences that quants are desperately trying to turn into mathematical pursuits. Savvy marketers go far beyond the numbers to touch the hearts and minds of consumers in ways that statistical formulas simply can't suggest.

14. Core values are always important to consider when marketing to Boomers. The problem is that it's impossible to pin down which combination of values is most important for a particular segment of the Boomer market. That's why it's best to treat the Boomers as a Market Segment Of One. Consider this. After googling a variety of sources, it appears that the following values are held by Americans 45 to 61 (listed from most to least important): altruism, family ties, intellectual curiosity, psychological well-being, spirituality, balance, leadership, civility,

warm relationships, excitement, regret, conservatism, recognition, national security. Another search provided these values held by Americans 62 and older (from most to least important): self-respect, family ties, faith and religion, warm relationships, kindness and compassion, intellectual curiosity, health and well being, fun and happiness, conservative attitudes, financial security, power and recognition, excitement, material possessions. Interesting perhaps, but painfully obvious. These searches provided nothing unique or insightful. In fact, you could have come up with these values simply by trusting your own insights.   In the final analysis, no matter how much core value research you do, this question remains: What do you do with this knowledge? How do you use these values to form the foundation of a communication platform that's not generic? The quants might be able to come up with formulas that make you feel more secure about any choices you make, but you can't quantify how to talk to Boomers person to person. That takes a special kind of creativity tempered by insights from gerontology counseling.

15. Most Boomers will be grandparents, and they're going

to love indulging the little ones quite generously in any number of ways. How can your brands get a piece of the action?

16. Let no popular idea or certain truth go unchallenged.

17. Never preach; instead, facilitate understanding.

18. Some Boomers feel that they are truly ageless. They don't deny their age; they just don't think about it. As a consequence, their outlook resembles that of idealistic youth that has been tempered by experience. These Boomers have a sharper sense of reality, taking what you might call a Zen approach to life. And this spirit goes well beyond New Age mumbo jumbo. It's a way of fully living in the present moment, and if your brands can devise a way to share that moment, it can be quite rewarding.

19. Good health means much more to Boomers than simple physical wellness. It is also firmly rooted in mental, emotional and spiritual well-being. That's why it pays to view Boomers holistically.

20. As Boomers age, they become more contemplative and discerning. They also tend to get down to the essence of things more quickly and efficiently by weeding out non-essential mental clutter. So if you want to communicate with them more effectively, remember that simplicity trumps complexity every time.

21. Effective marcom aimed at Boomers has a tone characterized by sincerity, authenticity, individualization and self-fulfillment.

22. As a group, the first Boomers entered adulthood by following serpentine paths of disobedience and confrontation with authority. To this day, the desire for dynamic opposition and conflict resolution is in every fiber of their collective character. Irrespective of political affiliations, their spirit of activism fundamentally supports inclusiveness and democratic processes.

23. Boomers have never stopped being young at heart, which is why they still enjoy a sense of adventure marked by highly individualistic, independent thinking and experimental behaviors.

24. There's a difference between looking older and living older. For instance, Mick Jagger has managed to smooth over the wrinkles of age with the vim and vigor of youthful exuberance, at least while on stage. How can your products and services provide a stage for Boomers to express themselves in a free and easy way? To get in the spirit of things, recall the brief nude scene at the end of Act I of *Hair.* Each night, the cast was given the choice to be in any state of undress or fully clothed, depending on the whim of the moment. Each actor took their own path to expressing themselves each evening. This is a small example of the love of individuality and freedom of expression that characterize the Boomer Generation.

25. Despite their avid consumerist tendencies, Boomers will lead the way toward simpler living. For convenience, they'll downsize their homes and wardrobes. They'll buy furniture that makes function fashionable. And they'll find greater fulfillment in the little things that they may have taken for granted. Of course, although they may come to believe that less is more, they won't accept substandard products or services.

26. As the Boomers inevitably face their own mortality, they will become far more interested in building a legacy that makes them feel that they will leave the world a better place.

27. When companies go overboard replacing human beings with technology, the quality of the customer experience diminishes. This especially rings true in customer service. A recorded voice that says, "Your call is very important to us" doesn't sound very convincing.

28. The demographic characteristics of the Boomer Generation will determine the course of American social and economic history for several decades, leaving a lasting imprint on this country that will never fade away.

29. The older the Boomer, the more crucial meaning becomes. These people expect more than a good standard of living; they expect to be able to live out their years with purpose. Nurturing this sense of meaningfulness is far more important than anything a mere fistful of dollars can buy. To discover the psychosocial dynamics behind your products and services, don't just ask "What does my

brand mean?" Ask "How does my brand mean?"

30. If you want to profit from the Boomers' increasing interest in meaning and purpose in later life, make Erik Erickson and Abraham Maslow your business partners. Their developmental theories will help you determine how you can convince Boomers that you offer something much more than just products and services. They'll also suggest ways that you can reposition your brands as genuine gateways to meaning and purpose in life.

31. As Boomers retire, how will they maintain a sense of usefulness without the daily structure of work? Will they engage in something traditional like volunteerism, or will they choose something far more creative? Something that is yet to be imagined?

32. How can you show Boomers that you value the highly individualized self-concepts and roles that they've developed?

33. How can you help Boomers convince themselves that their existence has mattered? What can you do to ensure

them that their legacy will endure?

34. The Boomers have always been big believers in word of mouth advertising. And because they grew up in the Age of Technology, they love staying connected via the Net, Facebook and Twitter. That means they have even more opportunities to influence the purchasing decisions of family and friends. Simply being there—on the Net, that is—can be good or bad, depending on how well you've branded your products and services. In assessing your branding, start with this question: Can I summarize my brand's Big Idea in a tweet that's only 140 characters long? If you can't do it, nobody else can, either.

35. History will judge America as a people based on how well we treat aging Boomers.

36. Current trends toward more impersonal forms of selling won't cut it with Boomers. They want to be heard and understood. They want their questions answered. And they want the benefits of your products and services clearly demonstrated in a compelling way.

37. Boomers will defeat negative images of aging by emphasizing an expanded concept of wellness, ultimately defining it as something much more than the mere absence of pathology. They will continue to find meaningful work. And they will enhance their psychosocial lives by using the latest technology to stay in closer touch with others, near and far. They will also remain a vital force in daily American life by actively participating in social and political movements, especially those that promise to either help or threaten them as individuals.

38. As always, Boomers will continue to be a disruptive social and economic force. By remaining true to their ways, they'll redefine what aging means for generations to come.

39. Quality of life is far more important to Boomers than mere longevity, which can be hellish without the benefits of Positive Aging.

40. The biotech innovations that Boomers embrace will be those that promise to increase the quality of their lives rather than those that prolong end-of-life suffering. That

means the next Viagra will be embraced much more readily than the next super-toxic form of chemotherapy. As proponents of Positive Aging, Boomers will continue to try to enjoy life to the fullest while developing the wisdom to know how to die just in the nick of time. Think of it as the reestablishment of *ars moriendi* for a death-denying America.

41. The Boomers' collective wisdom will help them realize that aging is not a disease that needs to be cured—that there can never be a drug or operation that can take the place of growing older in a realistic and graceful way. They will show the world that it's possible to age with dignity rather than desperation.

42. Boomers aren't set in their ways. Instead, they will create their own paths, just as they always have. They'll continue to be ambitious and driven, but in different ways and for new reasons.

43. Boomers aren't trying to freeze the hands of time by fantasizing about being young again. As life's clock ticks away, Boomers will be winding up for a big finish.

They like being responsible grownups who treasure their own special kind of beauty—the kind that can only come with aging gracefully and gratefully, both inwardly and outwardly.

44. Through Positive Aging, Boomers know that they can age well, deepening in complexity while building a unique legacy to leave their progeny and the world at large.

45. Free Love has never really gone out of style. Boomers are still sensual, sexual creatures, with a romantic spirit and lust for life.

46. To be sure, many Boomers are stuck in the challenging Sandwich Generation, but by and large, they know that they've lived the good life. That's why they're aging gratefully—generously giving their all for others.

47. Value is the new chic. Boomers still want luxury but at a sensible price.

48. Boomers are like the Wal-Mart of American generations because they're mega-consumers who know how to deal,

and they're hard bargainers, too. Wherever the Boomers show up, things get transformed.

49. Boomers can afford to buy more of everything than all the other demographic segments combined.

50. Boomers' needs and wants are continually evolving. That's why wise business leaders should expect the unexpected from this highly individualistic, often quirky bunch.

51. Along the way to building a tangible legacy, each Boomer also wants to gather fond memories from everything that they do.

52. The closer Boomers get to The End, the more they value time than money, and the more they would rather spend than save. In the final analysis, Boomers have no intention of dying on the cheap.

53. Hard sells don't work well with Boomers. You've got to listen carefully and speak to them in ways that they want to be spoken to.

54. Information triage is an unconscious process that controls the flow of information to the conscious mind based on its cumulative importance. To make the cut, information must be both relevant and emotionally stimulating. This means that if your marcom doesn't arouse the Boomer's emotions, the chance of its making a dent on the conscious mind approaches zero.

55. The feelings that your products and services conjure in the Boomer mind can be far more important than any of their more tangible features and benefits.

56. "Know thyself" is ancient wisdom "Know me," is contemporary wisdom, which recognizes that the Boomers take a "Hey, dig me!" approach to everyday life. Heeding their need for attention can really pay off.

57. Boomers can be very thoughtful shoppers, so once you've hooked them with an emotionally evocative message, they'll want more solid information than younger consumers before making a purchasing decision.

58. Inspiring images and testimonials that emphasize various

facets of Positive Aging will help your products and services gain entry to the Boomer Buying Center.

59. Vertically integrated, holistic communication campaigns build stronger brands because a multifaceted approach makes Boomers feel more completely understood, appreciated and respected.

60. Billboarding provocative ideas in bite-sized packages helps distill complex thoughts and emotions into terse messages that Boomers can easily wrap their minds around.

61. Almost all marketing communications sound like mono-logues. To effectively reach and persuade Boomers, you must make your marcom sound like an active dialogue. To do this, imagine what kinds of thoughts and feelings Boomers may have about your brand, and provide them with the kind of intelligent feedback that indicates that you've actually heard and understand them.

62. With each passing year, the Internet will become an increasingly important community for Boomers. As

a result, it will offer virtually unlimited potential for marketers to deliver detailed content to networked communities of like-minded people who value word of mouth advertising.

63. As Boomers continue to mature, they will seek higher quality experiences because they realize that time is running out.

64. "Quality of life" is a complex, highly individualized constellation of concepts that may include feelings of meaning and purpose, a discrete sense of self and more intimate connections to others, as well as physical, mental, emotional and spiritual well-being.

65. Boomers will show subsequent generations better ways to live and die.

66. No matter how tough the going gets, Boomers will continue to age gratefully, because they've reached many milestones that younger folks can only dream about. They'll also feel entitled to celebrate their successes, which they'll do right up to the very end.

67. Developing wisdom has a tremendous impact on psychological well-being, as well as spending habits. Most Boomers have the kind of mature mind that spends less time thinking about hip things to purchase and more time in the pursuit of buying experiences that truly enrich their everyday lives.

68. For the most part, Boomers have consistently enjoyed satisfying lives because they've developed qualities like self-sufficiency, self-confidence and the ability to survive tough times with more creativity than complaints. Overall, they are comfortable in their own skins, are able to relate well with others, and have come to terms with their own lives, warts and all.

69. Does your product empower Boomers? If so, exactly how? If not, how can you supercharge it with the kind of existential meaningfulness that goes far beyond mere utility? Discover and dramatize your brand's hidden magic and majesty, and you'll be welcomed into the Boomer Buying Center.

70. Boomers aren't close-minded, they're sure-minded.

71. If you overwhelm Boomers with your own point of view, they'll turn away from your products and services. But if you're relevant and interesting, they'll listen.

72. Authenticity rings true with Boomers, so don't try to persuade them using gimmicks like superficial imagery. Phoniness has all the emotional impact of clip art and stock photography.

73. Boomers are striving for genuineness in every aspect of their lives, so advertising and marcom that are insincere, dishonest or inaccurate are sure to offend and fail.

74. If you want to become Boomer-centric you must train yourself to understand and identify with what truly motivates Boomers of all ages.

75. Traditional consumer research is modeled after how minds and motivation work in the 18-49 demo. That's why it lacks the sensitivity and sensibility to provide reliable insights into the ways Boomers feel, think and make buying decisions. Younger mindsets tend to be more linear, literal and categorical. Boomer mindsets

are more subjective, individualistic and nuanced. Are the results of your research tuning in or turning off Boomers?

76. As Boomers have aged, their hedonistic self-indulgence has given way to responsible existential self-expression. They are now more concerned about making themselves fully conscious of the meaning of pleasurable experiences in a way that engages the total, unified self.

77. Studies have shown that Boomers perceive themselves to be up to fifteen years younger than they actually are. So far, the only thing that seems to have prevented any of them from feeling vital and vibrant is the misfortune of bad health, which is one reason why they take better care of themselves.

78. Boomers have led the way in establishing new spiritual values. As always, they've remained on the cutting edge by accepting diverse lifestyles and cultural traditions. They believe that developing inner strength is the key to taking personal responsibility for their lives. They've also shifted their spiritual emphasis from the dogmas of mainstream religions toward an openness to other

belief systems. On a more personal level, they have demonstrated a willingness to openly share their feelings even in the face of criticism. All of this has made them expansive in a way that's hard to define. That's why the best way to view them is as a Market Segment Of One.

79. As they seek greater spirituality, Boomers have made life a quest for continual growth—an exploratory journey of free choice, mindfulness, and integration of the diverse aspects of their existence.

80. As Boomers embrace the experience of growing older, they will integrate the concept of Positive Aging into their everyday values and behavior. This may result in a return to the idealism of their youth—an invigorating trip back in time that will be tempered by decades of experience and expertise in living.

81. Reframing is an important technique in cognitive-behavioral therapy. It can also be a potent motivational tool when used as the foundation for a sensitive marketing communication campaign. In that context, reframing can help redefine potential negative situations in a positive

way. For instance, you can reframe the final years of life as an opportunity to build a legacy that one can take pride in rather than as a path of inevitable disability and decline toward death.

82. Cognitive-behavioral therapy is a process that resembles a struggle between negative and positive thinking and decision making. It's actually much more than that, though. It's a way to help people marshal the personal resources required to make positive changes in their thinking and beliefs, which can lead to positive changes in their moods and behaviors. The process focuses on assessing and reframing deeply held beliefs that the client has about the self and the world at large. Deftly employed, cognitive-behavioral techniques can be used in marketing communications to help sway Boomers toward purchasing specific brands based on their perceived benefits.

83. To relate with the sensitivity of a counselor, you must learn to actively listen to Boomers. You must also regularly check their understanding of what you have to offer, and treat them with great respect and regard for their beliefs

and feelings. Of course, before you can hope to do all that, you must have a genuine and deep understanding of yourself, your company and your brands.

84. The counseling paradigm known as motivational interviewing suggests that effecting changes in buying behavior can't be imposed on Boomers. Instead, those changes must come from within. Various strategies, from simple persuasion to constructive confrontation, may help facilitate change, but in the end, you must identify and help mobilize each person's values and goals to help them move from ambivalence about your brand to actually buying it.

85. Ambivalence is a conflict between two or more courses of action (although it's usually considered a dichotomy). Each course is associated with its own perceived costs and benefits. If you're selling to Boomers, you must realize that it's their job, not yours, to resolve their natural ambivalence about whatever you're selling. You can give them all the best reasons in the world to buy, but only they can make the purchasing decision. For example, suppose you're selling a product that

helps people quit smoking. During the decision-making process, the prospect will likely have multiple inner conflicts to resolve that are confusing, contradictory and highly personal. The prospect's inner dialogue may go something like this: "If I stop smoking I'll feel better about myself and become healthier, but I might also gain weight, and that will make me feel fat, unattractive and less healthy." It's the marketer's job to understand the prospect's struggle and help that person make the journey from negativity through ambivalence and into making a positive purchasing decision.

86. Direct persuasion and logical arguments are seldom helpful in resolving ambivalence, because they usually increase the prospect's resistance, decreasing the probability of change. Instead, it's more effective to quietly facilitate the prospect's contemplative processes regarding the costs and benefits of change. The bottom line: You can't push prospects into buying, but you can gently coax them.

87. If you decide to use motivational interviewing techniques in your advertising and marcom, keep in mind that you

must help clarify and resolve the prospect's ambivalence in a respectful way that helps them overcome denial and resistance.

88. Motivational interviewing must strike a balance between being subtly directive and maintaining respect for the Boomer's autonomy. If it's perceived as a transparently manipulative technique, it will fail miserably.

89. As Boomers redefine what it means to grow older, age will become an obsolete marketing concept, and societal ageism will diminish, as well.

90. Boomers will continue to blossom in terms of creativity and intellectual development as they age. Their cumulative experience and expertise will encourage them to share their wisdom with younger people. Their vitality will keep them productive far longer than previous generations. And their compassion for others will be demonstrated in their concern for and work on behalf of the world at large.

91. If you think of Boomers as nothing more than self-ab-

sorbed, unpatriotic individualists, you probably also believe most of the other widely accepted negative images of aging. Boomers are unique, because in their hearts, they've never stopped experimenting with unconventional thinking and behavior. They still question and challenge arbitrary authority, and in doing so, they live in a world of their own making. The only certainly about the Boomers is their unpredictability. You must understand and respect their unflagging independence, or you'll never be accepted in the Boomer Buying Center.

92. If you can convince Boomers that you can custom-tailor a solution to their exact needs and desires, you'll create the confidence required for them to take a closer look at what you're selling.

93. Boomers have always loved to spend, and they don't scrimp, either. That doesn't mean they're easy marks, though. They're tough customers who won't buy anything that doesn't measure up to their high quality and high value standards.

94. Often, the perfect question is far more powerful than the

perfect statement, if it resonates deeply within the hearts and minds of Boomers.

95. Boomers have never believed in postponing gratification. Now that they hear Father Time's clock ticking more loudly, they're more likely than ever to spend freely.

96. Boomers are used to being risk takers, which is hardly surprising. After all, they grew up in a very perilous era marked by The Bomb, assassinations, burning cities, the draft, free love, Nixon and Watergate. They may become a bit more careful as they age, but they're not likely to shy away from risk—even the risk of running out of money.

97. Boomers are big on referring friends and family to products and services they like. Of course, the flipside is equally true. If you burn them, everybody in their circle will know about it in no uncertain terms. To stay on their good side, exceed their expectations, follow up with meticulous service, then stay in touch so you can build a library of testimonials to use in your marketing communications.

98. When seeking advice about marketing to Boomers, don't trust anyone under 50. Younger folks don't have the developmental experiences or sensibilities required to generate the kinds of concepts that can serve as a solid foundation for meaningful advertising and marcom campaigns directed at this unpredictable group. The root problem is that they're just too young to understand or give a damn, and they live in a very ageist society at a very ageist time. But change is in the air, and, to paraphrase Dylan, you don't need to be a weatherman to know which way the wind is blowin'.

99. What's the bigger challenge for your marketing messages: Cutting through the clutter of other communications that are competing for Boomers' attention, or breaking through the blandness of your own creative executions?

100. Boomers have already redefined what it means to be a teenager. They've done the some for what it means to be a twenty-, thirty-, forty- and fifty-something adult. Now they will redefine what it means to age beyond anyone's wildest expectations. Are you ready to take that trip with them into unexplored territory?

101. Want to chip away at any ageist tendencies you might harbor? Begin planning for your own hundredth birthday party today.